Reading Turkish Islamist Writers

Konstantinos Gogos

Reading Turkish Islamist Writers

N. F. Kısakürek, A. Bulaç, A. Dilipak

PETER LANG

**Bibliographic Information published by the
Deutsche Nationalbibliothek**
The Deutsche Nationalbibliothek lists this publication in the Deutsche
Nationalbibliografie; detailed bibliographic data is available online at
http://dnb.d-nb.de.

Library of Congress Cataloging-in-Publication Data
A CIP catalog record for this book has been applied for at the
Library of Congress.

ISBN 978-3-631-83006-2 (Print)
E-ISBN 978-3-631-83570-8 (E-PDF)
E-ISBN 978-3-631-83571-5 (EPUB)
E-ISBN 978-3-631-83572-2 (MOBI)
DOI 10.3726/b17599

© Peter Lang GmbH
Internationaler Verlag der Wissenschaften
Berlin 2020
All rights reserved.

Peter Lang – Berlin · Bern · Bruxelles · New York · Oxford · Warszawa · Wien

This publication has been peer reviewed.

www.peterlang.com

Table of Contents

Table of Contents 7

Prologue

This book is the English translation of my latest book, which was published in Greek in 2016 (by Livanis Puplications) and was intended to be used as a textbook for my students at the Department of Turkish Studies and Modern Asian Studies, National and Kapodistrian University of Athens. It introduces the writings and ideas of contemporary Turkish Islamist writers, and offers a perspective on the intellectual aspect of the Islamic movement in Turkey, an aspect which is relatively unknown outside Turkey. My principal goal and purpose when conceiving and writing this book was to combine a practical approach with a more theoretical one: in other words, to offer in translation some representative texts of the writers under study, and to discuss, though in a limited manner, the role of Islamist intellectuals in Turkey (and the Muslim world) as an alluring and engaging research topic.

As said above, this book was initially published in Greek—under the title "The Islamist movement in Turkey: Contribution to the study of contemporary Turkish Islamist thought." For the English-language version I have made only a few changes. Most of these changes concern the bibliography and quotations, as herein I use and refer to the original books published in English and not to their Greek translation or publication—as I did in the Greek version. On the other hand, it was necessary to translate into English (for the English-speaking reader) short or longer passages from the secondary Greek bibliography I used, something that was not needed in the Greek version.

Further, it should be noted that in the time that passed between the completion and publication of the original Greek-language book (in the first half of 2016) and the first months of 2019, when the English manuscript was completed, important political events and developments have occurred in Turkey that are related to at least one of the writers I refer to in the book. I have tried to refer to them and include them, when needed, in a synoptic and succinct way, without altering the structure of the book.

Initially, I translated the majority of the writings presented in the book from Turkish into Greek. For the English version the same writings have been translated into English. As far as Ali Bulaç is concerned, some of his writings were originally published in English and are therefore presented herein in their original form and style.

The difficult task of the English translation could not have been realized without the valuable assistance I received from a number of colleagues and professionals in the second half of 2018. I am deeply grateful to them; Sofia Bountouraki, who currently works as a translator at the Greek Translation Office of the EU in Luxemburg, translated major parts of the chapters dedicated to Ali Bulaç and Abdurrahman Dilipak; Maria Markopoulou, who is the Head of the Language Office of the International Award 'Giuseppe Sciacca' in Rome and a PhD candidate at the Sorbonne, translated the chapter dedicated to Necip Fazıl Kısakürek and copy-edited chapter 1; Anastassios Tsiropoulos, an English language teacher based in Athens, offered me his assistance in the translation of the Introduction and chapter 1; James Root, a recent MA graduate at the Center for Middle Eastern Studies, Lund University, Sweden, copy-edited the greater part of the manuscript and without doubt helped me to avoid mistakes and overcome difficulties in writing style and expression.

I must also thank my colleague Eylem Akdeniz Göker, Assistant Professor of Public Administration and Political Science at Altınbaş University in Istanbul, who read the introductory and theoretical parts of the manuscript and kindly shared with me her theoretical knowledge and perspective on the subject of intellectuals and society in Turkey. Her comments and remarks were crucial and fruitful. Last, but not least, I would like to thank my publishers for making this publication possible.

Needless to say I bear the sole responsibility for any mistake, inconsistency or misconception that may be found in the book, either in my argumentation and analysis or in the translation of the Turkish-language texts.

Konstantinos Gogos
Athens, March 2019

A Note on Pronunciation of Turkish Names

Throughout the book, I have used the Turkish language when mentioning names of persons, titles of books, and occasionally some terms. To assist the reader not familiar with the Turkish alphabet, here are some indications on pronunciation.

c sounds like the 'j' in job
ç sounds like the 'ch' in church
ğ soft g; not vocalized, lengthens the preceding vowel
ı (dotless I) sounds like the 'i' in cousin
ö sounds like the French 'eu'; like the German 'ö'
ş sounds like the 'sh' in shop
ü sounds like the French 'u'; like the German 'ü'

Introduction

The Importance of the Topic

The main purpose of this study is to contribute to the familiarization of the reader with the production of Islamist writers in contemporary Turkey, by focusing on the writings and ideas of three central figures in the Turkish Islamist movement: Necip Fazıl Kısakürek, Ali Bulaç, and Abdurrahman Dilipak.

All three belong to a circle of Islamist writers and intellectuals, a circle which plays a major protagonist role within the whole field of intellectual and literary production of contemporary Turkish intellectuals, as will hopefully become clear in the following chapters. Kısakürek was a prominent intellectual figure of the 20th century who engaged with various literary forms, history, philosophy, essay writing, as well as the publication of journals dedicated to the above-mentioned genres. The volume of his work, including that of religious or Islamist trends, meanings, and ideas, is immense. He can be classified as the pioneering Islamist and the intellectual father to the following generation of Islamist thought and activity in Turkey. It can also be claimed that Kısakürek, through his works, intertwines the late Ottoman Empire with the Turkey of the second half of the 20th century by bridging, spiritually and ideologically, the gap between the Ottoman intellectuals of the 19th century and contemporary Islamist intellectuals. On the other hand, both Bulaç and Dilipak are considered to be two of the most eminent and popular Islamist writers and intellectuals in present-day Turkey.

In addition, the present study seeks to contribute to the knowledge and understanding of the course of political Islam and the reinforcement of Islamic identity in Turkey, which emerged before 1980 and has since strengthened every following decade. The rise of political Islam in Turkey owes a great deal to the contribution of Islamist writers and intellectuals[1] who, through their writings, ideas, critiques, and suggestions, have led to the dissemination of an Islamic and Islamist view and interpretation of society, politics, economy, the state and its

---

1   As Thierry Zarcone stresses: "These intellectuals will exercise, in the last decades of the twentieth century and the beginning of the new millennium, by means of printed and especially visual medias, a remarkable influence on all classes of Turkish society, as well as on politics and the ruling parties." Thierry Zarcone, *La Turquie moderne et l' Islam* (Paris: Flammarion, 2004), 181. (My translation).

institutions, the culture and history of Turkey, the Muslim world, as well as the Western world in general.

This study focuses on the ideas and views of the three intellectuals on topics that are central to Islamist intellectuals. These specific topics could fall under the following—albeit thematically speaking general—labels: the Muslim world and Islam, history (from an Islamic, Ottoman, and Turkish viewpoint), politics, governing and ideology in modern Turkey (including notions such as democracy, Kemalism, reform, secularism, etc.), and Western civilization and the Western world.

In contrast with other topics or questions regarding the Muslim world or Islam, bibliographies about Islamist intellectuals are not particularly rich in Western languages and scholarly communities, even in those with a long tradition in Turkish and Islamic studies.[2] Naturally, the study of the ideas and the roles of Turkish Islamist writers and intellectuals has been more fruitful in Turkey in the last three decades, thanks to writers and scholars who mostly do not belong to the secular camp. The principal reason for this could be that secular writers, intellectuals, researchers, and university scholars in the fields of social and political sciences in Turkey failed to realize the phenomenon of Islamist intellectuals and writers in the 1980s and 1990s, the two decades crucial to its enhancement and expansion. It could even be claimed that many of them underestimated or even ignored its dimensions and dynamics.[3]

In terms of bibliography, this study is based on original Turkish texts of the three mentioned intellectuals (from books, essays, and articles), as well as on secondary literature including published and unpublished works in Turkish, English, Greek, and, to a much lesser degree, German and French.

As far as the structure of this book is concerned, a chapter is devoted to each of the three intellectuals. Each of these chapters contains biographical information, a short discussion of their main political views and ideas, as well as

---

2   Michael Meeker's essay remains a seminal and fundamental text for the study of contemporary Turkish Islamist intellectuals. See Michael M. Meeker, "The New Muslim Intellectuals in the Republic of Turkey," in *Islam in Modern Turkey: Religion, Politics and Literature in a Secular State*, ed. Richard Tapper (London: I. B. Tauris, 1991), 189–219. In Greece, Ioannis Mazis has touched upon this issue in his book *Mystical Islamic Orders and Political-Economic Islam in Contemporary Turkey* [in Greek] (Athens: Proskinio 2000), 171–79.

3   Among the secular scholars and academics who dealt with aspects of this issue relatively early, the names of Binnaz Toprak, Nermin Abadan-Unat, Nilüfer Göle, and Ayşe Kadıoğlu must be mentioned.

representative writings translated into English illustrating their Islamist thought, arguments, and writing style.

In addition, there is an introductory theoretical chapter with the purpose of placing the discussion of the emergence, role, and typology of Islamist intellectuals in Turkey, particularly in recent decades, in social theory terms and context. This chapter is intended to introduce the reader to theoretical and methodological aspects of the subject; it does not mean to be an exhaustive analysis of the relevant research and bibliography.

Clarification of Terms and Concepts

Before proceeding to the examination of the above, it is crucial that a clarification should be made regarding the two terms which are most frequently used in this study, the terms 'Islamist' and 'intellectual'. Over-simplistic though I may sound, I would like to explain in brief the way I perceive and use these two terms. I use the term 'Islamist' not as a synonym to 'Muslim', but rather to refer to those Muslims who choose either political or armed action, or write and theorize in favor of—or aiming at—the creation of a state and a society based upon and organized by Islam and its principles.[4] Islamists, whether writers, intellectuals, politicians, or armed fighters, comprise only a part of the entire Muslim population. They seek to Islamize, to restore, the rest of their society to the right and true Islam, which in turn they believe will result in their prosperity and puissance. In other words, as Ayşe Kadıoğlu has pointed out with regard to Islamists and political Islam: "Political Islam sees itself as having a political mission."[5] This is also how Roxanne L. Euben and Muhammad Qasim Zaman, editors of the volume *Princeton Readings in Islamist Thought* conceive and use the terms 'Islamism' and 'Islamist':

> We take 'Islamism' to refer to contemporary movements that attempt to return to the spiritual foundations of the Muslim community, excavating and reinterpreting them for application to the present-day social and political world. Such foundations consist of the Qur'an and the normative example of the Prophet Muhammad (*sunna; hadith*),

---

4   In other words: "Islamists try to find in Islam a political model able to compete with the most important Western ideologies." Ioannis Mazis, *Geography of the Islamist Movement in the Middle East* [in Greek], 3rd ed. (Athens: Papazisis, 2012), 50. (My translation).

5   Ayşe Kadıoğlu, "Women's Subordination in Turkey: Is Islam Really the Villain?" *Middle East Journal* 48:4 (Autumn 1994): 646.

which constitute the sources of God's guidance in matters pertaining to both worship and human relations.[6]

Additionally, they note that "Islamists may be characterized as explicitly and intentionally political and as engaging in multifaceted critiques of all those people, institutions, practices, and orientations that do not meet their standards of this divinely mandated political engagement."[7]

It has to be clear that although all Islamists pursue the same goal in general, the particular methods and means they choose to use can vary.[8] Having all the above in mind, I choose to speak about Islamist—and not about Muslim—politicians, activists, writers, or intellectuals.[9] However, other scholars have chosen a different approach. Michael Meeker has chosen to speak of 'Muslim' intellectuals arguing that this term—not the term 'Islamist'—is "preferred by these writers themselves" and that for them "the important point is that they write as believers, not that they write from an Islamic perspective. They therefore see themselves as Muslim rather than Islamist intellectuals. I have used the term Muslim intellectual in line with an anthropological preference for categories of self-reference."[10]

The term 'intellectual' is particularly difficult, if not impossible, to clarify or to determine in terms of meaning and context in an absolute manner, much less in a brief and concise one. Relevant literature on intellectuals, on who is an intellectual, and the role of intellectuals in Modern European societies and in the West in general, is rich in views of humanities scholars, social scientists,

---

6 *Princeton Readings in Islamist Thought: Texts and Contexts from Al-Banna to Bin Laden*, ed. Roxanne L. Euben and Muhammad Qasim Zaman (Princeton, NJ: Princeton University Press, 2009), 4.

7 Ibid.

8 This has been observed also by Kadıoğlu, who writes the following: "Political Islamists, furthermore, differ among themselves in their interpretation of this mission; some opt for participation directly in political power struggles to alter the existing system from above by capturing the state apparatus; others with a more populist tendency place primary emphasis on the individual and the means to transform gradually his/her internal value systems." Ayşe Kadıoğlu, "Women's Subordination," 646.

9 The term 'Islamist' is favored also by social scientists such as Ayşe Kadıoğlu, Nilüfer Göle, Cemil Aydın, Burhanettin Duran, and Michelangelo Guida. M. Hakan Yavuz prefers to speak about "Islamic" intellectuals or thinkers. See M. Hakan Yavuz, *Islamic Political Identity in Turkey* (New York: Oxford University Press, 2003), 112–21.

10 Michael M. Meeker, "The New Muslim Intellectuals," 189. Along this line, one can find scholars such as Ferhat Kentel, John Esposito, and John O. Voll.

and political-social philosophers who have dealt with this issue either directly or indirectly.[11]

The detailed discussion of the proposed terms, meanings, and theoretical framework of the complex issue of intellectualism and the social role of the intellectual is not the aim of this study. However, taking into account the existing bibliography, I would like to point out that I do not correlate the concept and the sociopolitical role of the intellectual strictly and only with progressive (whatever the meaning of the term 'progressive' may be), left/leftist, or revolutionary anti-establishment ideas in a society.

I tend to agree with Enzo Traverso's view that "the intellectual checks the authority, questions the dominant discourse, causes dissension, introduces a critical viewpoint"[12] and I can add what Stefanos Rozanis points out regarding the crucial significance of the act of writing of the intellectual: "the essential role of the intellectual as writer lies in the interpolation of writing in the socio-psychological, moral and political sphere."[13]

Moreover, a remark made by Edward Said is very helpful: "The central fact for me is, I think, that the intellectual is an individual endowed with a faculty for representing, embodying, articulating a message, a view, an attitude, philosophy or opinion to, as well as for, a public."[14] It is also worth mentioning that, according to Said:

> There is no such thing as a private intellectual, since the moment you set down words and then publish them you have entered the public world. Nor is there only a public intellectual, someone who exists just as a figurehead or spokesperson or symbol of a cause, movement or position. There is always the personal inflection and the private sensibility, and those give meaning to what is being said or written. Least of all should

---

11 Edward Said has offered a stimulating discussion of the meaning and the social role of the intellectual. See Edward W. Said, *Representations of the Intellectual: the 1993 Reith Lectures* (New York: Vintage Books, 1994). For a sociological perspective see Charles Kurzman and Lynn Owens, "The Sociology of Intellectuals," *Annual Review of Sociology*, 28 (2002): 63–90.

12 Enzo Traverso, *What Happened to the Intellectuals?* [in Greek], transl. Nikos Kourkoulos (Athens: Ekdoseis tou Eikostou Protou, 2014), 14. With regard to the development of the role of intellectuals in the Western world, Traverso notes "the transition from the old-type engaged intellectual who was a supporter of revolutionary affairs, an antifascist and anti-colonialist, to the new-type of intellectual whose political stand derives directly from his humanism." Ibid., 91. (My translation).

13 Stefanos Rozanis, *Intellectuals and Modernity* [in Greek] (Athens: Exarheia, 2015), 59. (My translation).

14 Edward W. Said, *Representations of the Intellectual*, 9.

an intellectual be there to make his/her audiences feel good: the whole point is to be embarrassing, contrary, even unpleasant.[15]

It should be noted, however, that Said clearly acknowledges that "the intellectual is a secular being"[16] and that he places emphasis on the role and responsibility of the secular intellectual.[17] Said further declares the following: "My argument is that intellectuals are individuals with a vocation for the art of representing, whether that is talking, writing, teaching, appearing on television. And that vocation is important to the extent that it is publicly recognizable and involves both commitment and risk, boldness and vulnerability."[18]

As far as the sociopolitical role of the intellectual is concerned, the understanding on which this study is based derives from a synthesis of the above-mentioned remarks and observations, with the emphasis on the intellectual's critical position and expression, his/her public discourse, and commitment to the public within a given society.

Academic research and discussion on intellectuals in the Muslim world does not boast the rich bibliography published about intellectuals in the Western world. Research on intellectuals in contemporary Muslim societies is a lot more recent; academic research and theoretical involvement with either Islamic (religious) or Islamist (political-ideological) intellectual production has mainly developed in the last three decades.

---

15 Ibid., 9–10.
16 Ibid., 89.
17 He notes: "Indeed I would go so far as saying that the intellectual must be involved in a lifelong dispute with the guardians of sacred vision or text, whose depredations and whose heavy hand brooks no disagreement and certainly no diversity." Edward W. Said, *Representations of the Intellectual*, 65.
18 Ibid., 10.

Chapter 1 Islamist Intellectuals in Turkey: Introductory and Theoretical Observations

The Emergence of Contemporary Islamist Intellectuals

The formation, role, and appeal of Islamist intellectuals in Muslim societies has been central to research and studies on Islam and the Muslim world since the 1990s. While in pre-modern Muslim societies the distinction between traditional religious scholars of Islamic law (called *ulema*) and secular scholars of literature and science (namely poets, writers, philosophers, and scientists) is quite clear, in the modern era, and particularly since the 19th century, the profile of secular thinkers who support modern Western-type reforms has been enhanced.

At the same time a new trend has emerged and has gradually been strengthened: Muslim intellectuals who are not *ulema* (but are mostly staunch adversaries of them), who oppose Western-type reforms and secularization. More specifically, they advocate the revival of Islam from within and propose specific sociopolitical actions towards this aim.

The 19th century Ottoman Empire is a remarkable example of conflict and struggle between (secular and positivist) modernists and Islamists over ideas and political practices. It was also the breeding ground of three different wider groups and intellectual poles: one consisting of the traditional dogmatic *ulema*, a second of modernist secular intellectuals, and a third of anti-secular intellectuals who preached the revival and reinforcement of Islam (Islamists) through its own spirit and powers.[19]

Exactly this specific type of anti-secular, anti-Western Islamist intellectual started to gain more significance and visibility in 20th century Muslim societies – within the social, political, economic, and geopolitical conditions of the century.

---

19 For a detailed account of the ideological and intellectual currents in the late Ottoman Empire, see Niyazi Berkes, *The Development of Secularism in Turkey*, with a new intoduction by Feroz Ahmad (New York: Routledge, 1998), 64–428. A brief account is offered by M. Şükrü Hanioğlu, *A Brief History of the Late Ottoman Empire* (Princeton: Princeton University Press, 2008), 94–104, 138–44, and 183–88. For more about the Islamist thinkers of that period and their ideas, see Ahmet Şeyhun, *Islamist Thinkers in the Late Ottoman Empire and Early Turkish Republic* (Leiden: Brill, 2014).

These Islamist intellectuals are also referred to as "Muslim activist intellectuals" by John L. Esposito and John O. Voll,[20] or "Islamic revivalists" by Ali Rahnema.[21]

In particular, regarding the significance and enhancement of the Islamist intellectual's social role in the second half of the 20th century, and most importantly in the last 30 years of the century, I have noted in the past "their decisive contribution to the forging of a demanding, thinking, and educated Muslim (religious) public in various areas of the Muslim World."[22] This social and cultural evolution of intellectuals and writers in the Muslim world has also been emphasized by Dale Eickelman, who observes that:

> A new sense of public is emerging throughout Muslim-majority states and Muslim communities elsewhere. Joined with this new sense of public are new intellectual styles and messages, disseminated in increasingly diverse yet overlapping fields of communication and understanding. The influence of state authorities and intellectuals trained in the formal religious sciences remain strong, but their authority is increasingly displaced by intellectuals with increasingly disparate backgrounds.[23]

Eickelman also points out that "for such Muslim-majority countries as Indonesia and Turkey, religious intellectuals play a major role in furthering the goals of civil society, religious pluralism, and tolerance."[24] Indeed, the development and appeal of Islamist thought in the last decades is obvious in many societies and countries of the Muslim world, particularly in those which more often than not are considered to have a leading ideological and cultural role, such as Indonesia, Turkey, Egypt, and Iran.

As to the discussion regarding Islamist intellectuals, Farhad Khosrokhavar in his study on the intellectuals in Shia Iran makes a distinction between "revolutionary intellectuals" and "reformist or the so-called 'post-Islamist intellectuals.'"[25]

---

20 See John L. Esposito and John O. Voll, *Makers of Contemporary Islam* (New York: Oxford University Press, 2001), 20–22.

21 See Ali Rahnema, ed., *Pioneers of Islamic Revival*, new updated ed. (London: Zed Books, 2005), 4–10.

22 Konstantinos Gogos, "Turkish Islamist intellectuals and the Islamist movement: the view of Ali Bulaç" [in Greek], in *Tourkologika*, ed. G. Salakidis (Thessaloniki: Ant. Stamoulis, 2011), 423.

23 Dale F. Eickelman, "Clash of Cultures? Intellectuals, their publics, and Islam", in *Intellectuals in the Modern Islamic World: Transmission, Transformation, Communication*, eds. Stephane A. Dudoignon, Komatsu Hisao, and Kosugi Yasushi (London: Routledge, 2006), 289.

24 Ibid., 290.

25 Farhad Khosrokhavar, "The New Intellectuals in Iran", *Social Compass*, 51:2 (2004): 195.

According to him, Shariati, Khomeini, and Motahhari constitute "the first generation of Islamist Intellectuals" and belong to the first category, while Abdolkarim Soroush, Mojtahed Shabestari, Mostafa Malekian, Mohsen Kadivar, and Yousefi Eshkavari belong to the latter group.[26] Clearly this is a typology that is based on the dilemma of the support of revolutionary action and (revolutionary) political change whose aim is an Islamic society and government.

Moreover, with regard to the Iranian case, Khosrokhavar characterizes as "intermediary intellectuals" a group of intellectuals and writers, of the present and recent generations, who usually work as journalists and disseminate ideas and opinions of the "grand intellectuals"—that is, the distinguished intellectuals with international appeal, such as Soroush and Shabestari. As he writes:

> They spread the ideas of the promoters of reformist Islam and they inaugurate a new style of intellectualism which, combining journalism and abstract ideas, has its own distinctive features. [. . .] But the new style of intellectualism inaugurated by journalists is sociologically separate from the "grand intellectuals", although its thought takes inspiration from them, but it holds to its own course and trend.[27]

Furthermore, many social scientists and researchers adopt the term "public intellectual" for those intellectuals who have emerged in the last decades and whose main feature is public speech, the expression of their opinions and argumentation through the press, essays, participation in mass media programs, or on the internet. This happens on a very frequent basis, since for many of these intellectuals publishing essays and books, or working as magazine and newspaper editors, is their livelihood.

In order to understand the historical and social frame of the emergence of contemporary Islamist intellectuals in the Muslim world, the viewpoint of sociologist Nilüfer Göle is worthy of consideration. According to Göle, Islamist intellectuals are part of the second phase of the Islamist movement "whereby a cultural program of Islam becomes more apparent."[28] Göle holds that the Islamist movement is marked by two distinct phases and explains:

> The first phase, which reached its peak with the Iranian Revolution of 1979, created a model for Islamization throughout the 1980s. During this phase, Islamic public ac tion was mostly defined by militant fundamentalists thinking in revolutionary terms.

---

26 Ibid., 195–96.
27 Ibid., 194–95.
28 Nilüfer Göle, "Islamic Visibilities and Public Sphere," in *Islam in Public: Turkey, Iran, and Europe*, eds. Nilüfer Göle and Ludwig Amman (Istanbul: Istanbul Bilgi University Press, 2006), 4.

In contradistinction, in its second phase, it is new social groups such as Muslim intellectuals, cultural elites, entrepreneurs, and middle classes that more greatly define the public face of Islam, thinking and acting in reformist terms. Their social profiles are an outcome of both the Islamist movement and modern secular education, market values and political idioms. They are a hybrid and embody to the extreme the ambivalence between Islam and modernity; they make a claim for Islamic difference, and yet accept certain imperatives of modern life. They are disenchanted with the utopian fundamentalism that Islamist militants cherished two decades ago and seek to make a place for themselves in professional, political and public life.[29]

As Göle stresses, although the new generations of Islamists have shifted the dynamics and orientation of the Islamist movement, "this does not mean the end of radicalism, which increasingly manifests itself in terrorist acts."[30] On the other hand, she argues that "today Muslim identity is in the process of 'banalization'" and, more specifically, explains:

Hence, we observe a transformation of these movements from a radical political stance to a more social and cultural orientation, accompanied by a loss of mass mobilization and populist fervor. Some researchers wanted to deduce from this the "decline of Islamism" or the "failure of political Islam." But a more cultural orientation does not mean a less political one. Indeed, from our perspective, Islam, instead of disappearing as a reference, penetrates even more deeply into the social fiber and imaginary, thereby raising new political questions, not addressed solely to Muslims but also concerning the principles of collective life in European and Western context.[31]

Göle is here referring to the conclusions and views of Olivier Roy and Gilles Kepel. Furthermore, she emphasizes the "creation of new public spaces and markets" and the crucial role played by "new Muslim youth, intellectuals, middle class and professional groups."[32]

I believe—as I have argued in the past—that the view expressed by Olivier Roy, according to which political Islam has failed, is (and was) lacking adequate and solid grounds.[33] On the contrary, I am of the opinion that there has been an

---

29 Ibid.
30 Ibid.
31 Ibid., 5–6.
32 Ibid., 6.
33 See my argumentation in Konstantinos Gogos, "Political Islam in the Middle East: A Story of Failure or Success?" [in Greek], in *Proceedings of the 1st Middle Eastern Conference of the National and Kapodistrian University of Athens: 10–12 December 2012*, ed. Ioannis Mazis and Kyriakos Nikolaou Patragas (Athens: Leimon, 2013), 57–69.

evident rise and success of political Islam in Turkey as well as in other Muslim countries.

Turkish Islamist Intellectuals and Social Theory

This study seeks to shed light on the work of contemporary Turkish Islamist intellectuals, as they constitute a significant pillar of the Islamist movement, which in many cases can be considered as the ideological and cultural vanguard of it. It focuses on their views and ideas, aiming to showcase their contribution to the development and (re-)formation of the contemporary Islamist movement in Turkey.

From a sociological point of view, using the concepts of Pierre Bourdieu, it can be claimed that these writers and intellectuals have succeeded in shaping and strengthening the "cultural capital" of the Islamist movement, which has decidedly contributed to the strengthening of the Islamist movement and has expanded its political power. In other words, we can say that Islamist intellectuals, and the media in which they write and express their opinions (magazines, newspapers, publications, television and radio programs, internet, lectures, and institutes), have created, since it began to flourish in Turkey in the 1980s, a strong and rising cultural capital: a form of capital which the Islamist movement of previous decades lacked to a large extent. This cultural capital has been added to the political, financial, and social capital the Islamist movement already possessed or claimed, and has positively influenced it. In the case of Turkey, in my view, this cultural capital paved the way towards the social infusion and political-electoral success of the Islamist movement.

If we examine the Turkish Islamist movement and Turkish society using theoretical tools and concepts proposed by Bourdieu, we can say that the field of literary production (or literary field), which encompasses not only literature but also other forms of literary production such as journalistic texts, essays, or studies, constitutes one of the social fields of contemporary Turkey. In any given society, the literary field belongs to the wider field of cultural production.[34] In each field its members compete against each other, either as individuals or as groups, in order to improve their status by using one or more forms of capital: financial, social, cultural, or symbolic.[35]

---

34 For more see Pierre Bourdieu, *The Field of Cultural Production: Essays on Art and Literature* (Cambridge: Polity Press, 1993).

35 About the forms of capital, see Pierre Bourdieu, "Social Space and Symbolic Power," *Sociological Theory* 7:1 (Spring 1989): 14–25; Pierre Bourdieu, "The Forms of Capital," in *Readings in Economic Sociology*, ed. Nicole Woolsey Biggart (Oxford: Blackwell

Under these terms, it can be said that in the first decades of the Turkish Republic,[36] the field of cultural production and, more specifically, the field of literary and written production, was occupied, shaped, and demarcated almost exclusively by writers and intellectuals of Kemalist ideology and worldview. That is, they exhibited strong tendencies towards Turkish nationalism, Western modernization, secularism, statism, and authoritarian rule.

In the first decades of the Turkish Republic the participation of writers who expressed different views or social standpoints was very limited in this field. This changed in the course of time through the socioeconomic changes experienced in Turkey. Starting in the 1970s, and particularly in the 1980s onwards, the writers of the Islamist movement developed their own expression and presence, while Islamist and Islamic publications multiplied. The participation and production of Islamist writers and intellectuals in the literary field increased progressively, leading to the decline of Kemalist writers, and the limiting of their dominant role in this particular field. Obviously, this participation boosted Islamists in their conflicts with Kemalists in different fields of the social world.

Göle has used Bourdieu's concept of "cultural capital"[37] and has stressed the crucial role which Islamist intellectuals played in Turkey: "As producers of symbols and values, Islamist intellectuals, such as Ali Bulaç, Ismet Özel, and Abdurrahman Dilipak, define and transmit the ideology of the Islamist movement through newspapers, periodicals and books."[38]

Now let us focus on the three intellectuals under study, by making use of the above-mentioned concepts and observations and aiming to demonstrate the contribution of Islamist intellectuals and writers in the shaping of the Islamist movement in Turkey. The first of them, Necip Fazıl Kısakürek, was a true pioneer

---

Publishers, 2002), 280–91; Pierre Bourdieu, *Raisons pratiques: Sur la théorie de l' action* (Paris: Editions du Seuil, 1994).

36 The Turkish Republic was established on October 29, 1923 and Mustafa Kemal was its first President.

37 Nilüfer Göle wrote almost two decades ago about "the contemporary debate between Islamism and secularism from the perspective of the formation and circulation of elites and counter-elites. The concept of elite is used here to refer to those new social groups such as intellectuals and the technical intelligentsia (engineers and technicians) which, through secular and modern education, have acquired a "cultural capital", namely a universal scientific language and professional skills." Nilüfer Göle, "Secularism and Islamism in Turkey: The Making of Elites and Counter-Elites," *Middle East Journal* 5:1 (Winter 1997): 46–47.

38 Ibid., 56.

and representative of Islamism in the literary field during the first decades of the Turkish Republic, when it was dominated by Kemalist writers and intellectuals. He has inspired many Islamist as well as conservative intellectuals and politicians of younger generations.

Ali Bulaç and Abdurrahman Dilipak are two "critical figures of the Islamic movement in Turkey", as Ayşe Kadıoğlu has pointed out.[39] Indeed, both of them are prolific writers who play a major role in the expression, shaping, and strengthening of the cultural capital of the Islamist movement in contemporary Turkey. It is important to mention that despite having common points of reference and a common starting point, their views do not always coincide; as a matter of fact they may sometimes differ significantly. The following example should be quite explanatory. Dilipak often criticizes and denounces Fethullah Gülen and his community, attacking not only Gülen but also his supporters and publications because he believes they aim to create a "parallel structure" at the expense of the Turkish state and people. Dilipak is in favor of the policies and actions of the ruling (Justice and Development) party against the Gülen community. On the other hand, Bulaç, who was a columnist in the daily newspaper *Zaman,* a pro-Gülen newspaper, often criticized the same party and government for their decisions and policies which not only aimed at containing the Gülen community and its activities, but also (he claimed) at reducing any opposition voices.

In a way, Dilipak is seen as the true voice of the political dimension of the Islamist movement, whereas Bulaç is the voice of the cultural dimension of it. According to Göle, the former expresses "political Islamism", while the latter expresses "cultural Islamism."[40] As explained by Menderes Çınar and Ayşe Kadıoğlu "Bulaç is a cultural Islamist for he does not believe in participating directly in political power struggles in order to alter the existing system from above by capturing the state apparatus, but rather places a significance on the individual and the means to transform gradually his/her internal value systems."[41]

According to this distinction, political Islamism—or the political dimension of Islamism—emphasizes political action and activism aiming at the seizure of political power and state institutions. From this perspective, Islamization of

---

39 Ayşe Kadıoğlu, "Women's subordination in Turkey: Is Islam really the villain?" *Middle East Journal* 48:4 (Autumn 1994): 646, footnote 3.

40 As Göle observed in the 1990s. See Nilüfer Göle, *The Forbidden Modern: Civilization and Veiling* (Ann Arbor: The University of Michigan Press, 1996), 109.

41 Menderes Çınar and Ayşe Kadıoğlu, "An Islamic Critique of Modernity in Turkey: Politics of Difference Backwards," *ORIENT* 40:1 (1999): 54.

individuals and society develops as a top-down process. Cultural Islamism—or the cultural dimension of Islamism—prioritizes the creation of a strong Islamic identity and consciousness in individuals and society through cultural, educational, social, and charitable activities. In this case, Islamization of the state and its institutions will only be feasible as a result of the Islamization of individuals and society; in other words, Islamization occurs as a bottom-up process.[42]

Nonetheless, it should be said that it is very difficult to draw an evident and permanent dividing line between the cultural and the political expression of Islamism. This is not only because in any given contemporary society the political is intertwined with the cultural and the social, but also because, in the case of Islamism, what substantially matters is the aim to achieve an Islamic state and society, and an Islamic way of life. This aim is common to all Islamists. In this regard, I agree with Eylem Akdeniz Göker who notes:

> The clear categorical cut between 'cultural' and 'political' Islamism is problematic. Any given form of Islamism will rather have various 'degrees' of cultural and political forms of expression. Depending on where the movement – or even, where a given intellectual– stands in the field of power (leaning towards the dominant or the dominated), there will be tactical choices between using cultural or political 'tools'.[43]

---

42   In the words of Göle: "In contrast to political Islam, which advances confrontation with the "system," cultural Islam is the conveyor of a new value system. Laying the bases of the movement with the assistance of the "Muslim personality and identity", before all else it advocates "complete independence in the mental world." Questioning the inherent tensions between Islam and politics, tradition and modernism, religion and profanity, belief and rationalist positivism, this movement locates the conflict between Islam and the West on a new intellectual axis." Nilüfer Göle, *The Forbidden Modern*, 110.

43   Eylem Akdeniz Göker, oral communication with me (October 28, 2018). Eylem Akdeniz Göker is an Assistant Professor of Political Science and Public Administration at Altınbaş University in Istanbul.

Chapter 2 Necip Fazıl Kısakürek

In his novel "Snow", Orhan Pamuk—winner of the 2006 Nobel Prize in Literature—creates a number of characters belonging ideologically and socio-politically to the Turkish Islamist movement. Each character expresses and represents a different type of Islamist thought and action. Among these characters, we meet Necip and Fazil, two young students that attend an Islamic religious institution (*Imam Hatip* school). It is possible that the choice of these names by Orhan Pamuk was not a coincidence, as they might refer to the prominent Turkish poet, novelist, essayist, and political theorist, Necip Fazıl Kısakürek, an intellectual who has strongly influenced the Islamist thought and literature of contemporary Turkey.

Short Biography

Necip Fazıl Kısakürek was born on May 26th, 1905, in the Çemberlitaş quarter of Istanbul. He died on May 25th, 1983, in Erenköy, Istanbul. His father, Abdülbaki Fazıl Bey, had studied law and held various positions as a judge and a prosecutor; his mother, Mediha, originated from a family that had come to Istanbul from Crete. Necip Fazıl's grandfather (from his father's side) was probably the most significant figure in the household; Mehmet Hilmi Efendi[44] was a retired judge of the criminal court and a member of the committee that drafted the Ottoman Civil Code (*Mecelle*).[45] Necip Fazıl's grandmother Zafer also came from a highly respected family, being the daughter of Salim Paşa, who had served as province governor (*vali*) in Aleppo and as Secretary of the Ministry of Foreign Affairs.[46]

Thus it becomes obvious that Necip Fazıl was a 'genuine child' of the social and cultural conditions of the last decades of the Ottoman Empire, given that he grew up in a family circle consisting of educated administrative and judicial functionaries. In addition, his path of education reflected the educational structures of that period. Necip Fazıl enrolled in more than one public school,

---

44 Originating from the province of Kahramanmaraş, known also as Maraş. See M. Orhan Okay, *Necip Fazıl Kısakürek* (Ankara: Kültür ve Turizm Bakanlığı Yayınları, 1987), 1.

45 Ibid. *Mecelle*, the Ottoman Civil Code consisted of 16 volumes and was drawn up between 1869 and 1876. For more, see Niyazi Berkes, *The Development of Secularism*, 168–69.

46 Muzaffer Uyguner, *Necip Fazıl Kısakürek: Yaşamı, Sanatı, Yapıtlarından Seçmeler* (Ankara: Bilgi Yayınevi, 1994), 9.

including an American one until 1913 when his family moved to the island of
Heybeliada (Halki), not far from Istanbul, where he completed his primary education. He then entered the Naval School from which he graduated in 1920.[47]

These formative years were of great significance for his future development, as
he wrote his first poems and was taught by a number of preeminent teachers such
as Yahya Kemal Beyatlı, Hamdullah Suphi Tanrıöver, Aksekili Ahmed Hamdi,
and İbrahim Aşki Tanık,[48] all of whom played an important role in the intellectual and political life of Turkey. It should be mentioned that the first two were
among the proponents of Turkish nationalism, while the latter two represented
Islam and the Islamic spirit, either in its mystical or in its state dimension. As a
matter of fact, in both his work and political life, one can spot ties to the ideological currents of Islamism and Turkish nationalism, although Kısakürek apparently attached more importance to Islam and Islamic mysticism.

In 1921, Necip Fazıl began to study philosophy at the Darülfünun,[49] and in 1924
he received a state scholarship to study philosophy at the Sorbonne University
in Paris, becoming one of the first students to be sent abroad by the newly established Turkish Republic. In 1922, during his time at university, Kısakürek's first
poems were published in the literary magazine *Yeni Mecmua* (New Magazine),
one of the most important publications of the newly emerging Turkish literary
and intellectual scene at that time. In Paris, he was highly attracted to the Parisian
life and did not turn out to be a committed and diligent student.[50] As a result,
he returned to Turkey before finishing his degree. Kısakürek's Parisian period

---

47 Ibid., 8. See also M. Orhan Okay, *Necip Fazıl Kısakürek*, 2.
48 See M. Orhan Okay, *Necip Fazıl Kısakürek*, 2. It is worth adding very briefly the fol-
    lowing short biographies: Yahya Kemal Beyatlı (1884–1958) was a poet, teacher of
    culture and literature, essayist, journalist, and a proponent of Turkish nationalism and
    the Young Turks. For a number of years he was a member of parliament and served
    as a diplomat abroad. Hamdullah Suphi Tanrıöver (1885–1966) was a writer, teacher,
    and nationalist intellectual who was a member of the parliament for many years, and
    he served as Minister for Education (for a few months in 1925) and as Ambassador to
    Bucharest (1931–1944). Aksekili Ahmed Hamdi was a prominent theologian, who held
    the post of the President of the Diyanet İşleri Başkanlığı, the state-controlled Presidium
    for Religious Affairs, from 1947 until his death. İbrahim Aşki Tanık (1874–1977) was
    a teacher of Ottoman Literature and one of the first persons who opened the window
    of the mystical Islamic spirit to Kısakürek.
49 The Ottoman Higher Education institution, meaning "House of Sciences". The
    University of Istanbul was established as its successor in 1933.
50 M. Orhan Okay, *Necip Fazıl Kısakürek*, 2. In other words, he was attracted by the
    drinking, the gambling, the company of women, and the Bohemian lifestyle.

can, however, be characterized as a milestone in his intellectual and ideological maturation. In Paris, he met the philosopher Henri-Louis Bergson and was considerably influenced by him. Furthermore, while in Paris, the young Necip Fazıl experienced a deep intellectual crisis and drew conclusions that formed his own view and conception of the Western civilization: a civilization in decay which continuously experiences crises.[51]

After his return from Paris in 1926, Kısakürek was employed by banks in different Turkish cities, while from time to time he taught in various educational establishments.[52] In the meantime he published poetry and prose. From 1931 to 1932 he served in the military, and in 1941 he married Fatma Neslihan Baban, daughter of a long-established family, with whom he had five children (born from 1943 to 1954).[53] In 1942 Necip Fazıl decided to exclusively dedicate himself to his writing and publishing activities.[54]

Kısakürek's Publishing Activities

In order to impart his ideas and strengthen the ideologization of Islam, Kısakürek originally published the journal *Ağaç* (Tree) and, a few years later, the journal *Büyük Doğu* (Great East). As M. Hakan Yavuz makes very explicit, the aforementioned journals "played a primary role in the politicization of the Islamic identity."[55]

---

51 In other words, a civilization "condemned to hit its head against one wall after another and play hide and seek from one crisis after another" as stated in Burhanettin Duran, *Transformation of Islamist Political Thought in Turkey from the Empire to the Early Republic (1908-1960): Necip Fazil Kisakürek's Political Ideas* (PhD diss., Bilkent University, Ankara 2001), 204. Duran refers to a passage of Kısakürek's work "O ve Ben" [Him and Me] and its English translation from Şerif Mardin, "Culture Change and the Intellectual: A study of the Effects of Secularization in Modern Turkey: Necip Fazıl and the Nakşıbendî", in *Cultural Transitions in the Middle East*, ed. Şerif Mardin (Leiden: Brill, 1994), 189-213.

52 Such as the Higher State Conservatoire in Ankara, the Faculty of Language, Literature and Geography of the University of Ankara, the State Academy of Arts in Istanbul, and the former Robert College (Bosphorus University) in Istanbul. See M. Orhan Okay, *Necip Fazıl Kısakürek*, 2; *Doğumunun 100. Yılında Necip Fazıl Kısakürek 1904-1983* (Istanbul: İstanbul Büyükşehir Kültür Yayınları, n.d.), 22.

53 *Doğumunun 100. Yılında*, 12-22.

54 M. Orhan Okay, *Necip Fazıl Kısakürek*, 3.

55 M. Hakan Yavuz, *Islamic Political Identity*, 116.

The weekly *Ağaç*, which began publishing in 1936, aspired to offer its readership a perspective completely different from the materialist and Kemalist view of the majority of the printed publications in Turkey at the time. Kısakürek's goal was primarily to enable the expression of the intellectual and artistic concerns and doubts of that time, as opposed to the dominant idealization of the reformist and materialist tendencies in literature, aesthetics, and the intelligentsia of the Kemalist regime.[56] In other words, it sought to provoke reflection and criticism about the course of the young Turkish Republic and the imposition of Kemalist reforms. While important Turkish writers and intellectuals wrote for the magazine,[57] *Ağaç* did not receive the desired recognition amongst the public. Together with its financial problems, the magazine's publication was brought to an end right after its seventeenth issue.[58]

In spite of his unsuccessful publishing attempt, Necip Fazıl did not abandon the idea of publishing a review, which would be the expression of his ideas and reflections. After a few years, and since he had found, in the meantime, shelter for his texts in the press,[59] he decided to start *Büyük Doğu,* which was first published in September 1943. Its significance lies not only in the texts it published, but also in the fact that it is one of the longest-lasting magazines in modern Turkey. *Büyük Doğu* experienced occasional interruptions of publication and changes in the frequency of circulation until its last print on June 14th, 1978. During this thirty-five-year period, after its initial release as a weekly publication, it was sometimes released as a monthly or daily newspaper. *Büyük Doğu* often became a target of the police and the judicial authorities, which closed down the magazine, as well as imprisoned Kısakürek. Indeed, he was forced to close his own publication several times in order to avoid worse measures.

It is noteworthy that *Büyük Doğu*, in different phases of its publication,[60] contained different material or subject matters. To understand this diversity, it should be mentioned that during the first year of the journal's circulation, until its closure in May 1944, its subject matters were mainly of political interest, and references to the World War were not missing. In the very next phase of its

56 M. Orhan Okay, *Necip Fazıl Kısakürek*, 5.
57 Such as: Ahmet Hamdi Tanpınar, Ahmed Kudsi, Burhan Toprak, Abdülhak Şinasi Hisar, Mustafa Şekip Tunç, Sabahattin Ali, Sait Faik, Bedri Rahmi Eyüboğlu. See M. Orhan Okay, *Necip Fazıl Kısakürek*, 5.
58 Ibid.
59 Namely in the newspapers *Haber* (News), and *Son Telgraf* (Last Telegram). Ibid.
60 For more about the periods of its publication see M. Orhan Okay, *Necip Fazıl Kısakürek*, 15–18.

circulation, from November 1945 to May 1948, the journal was characterized by a greater number of writers and a greater diversity in subject matters, including art, philosophy, literature, and politics. In the third phase of its release, from March 1949 to August 1949, the journal did not publish any texts on literature or art. Finally, in the fourth phase of its publication, from October 1949 to June 1951, *Büyük Doğu* was more politically and religiously orientated.[61]

Kısakürek's publishing activities also include another short-lived publication released in November and December 1947. This was a weekly newspaper named *Borazan*, which contained numerous texts written by Necip Fazıl that expressed political and social satire.[62]

Kısakürek's political activity

The material and priorities of the journal *Büyük Doğu* in its different publishing periods reflect, to a great extent, the intellectual world, the interests, and the political thought of its publisher. From the beginning of the 1950s and after, Necip Fazıl became more defiant and critical in political and religious issues, not only through his writings but also through his relations with political parties and politicians. During these years (from 1946 and after), Turkey was making steps towards political polyphony and democracy, as the transition from the single-party to the multi-party system took place. In the elections of May 1950, the Democratic Party (DP: *Demokrat Parti*), which was founded in 1946, defeated the Republican People's Party (CHP: *Cumhuriyet Halk Partisi*), which had been in power since the foundation of the Turkish Republic.

In these advantageous circumstances for political polyphony, in 1949 Kısakürek founded the political organization *Büyük Doğu* (*Büyük Doğu Cemiyeti* – Great East Association), which in 1951 was forced to interrupt its service by judicial authority after having created local offices in seven cities.[63]

Despite the fact that Kısakürek showed fondness towards the Democratic Party, which was giving more attention to the religious sentiments of the citizens, and ideologically was more conservative than the Republican People's Party, his relationship with the Menderes government was not always good. The position of Prime Minister Adnan Menderes and his government on Kısakürek

---

61 Ibid., 16–17. Its last phase of circulation took place between May 8 and June 5, 1978.
62 Ibid., 18–19.
63 See Michelangelo Guida, "Founders of Islamism in Republican Turkey: Kısakürek and Topçu", in *Intellectuals and Civil Society in the Middle East: Liberalism, Modernity and Political Discourse*, ed. Mohammed A. Bamyeh (London: I. B. Tauris, 2012), 117.

(and his journal *Büyük Doğu*) was ambivalent for political reasons, oscillating between tolerance, support,[64] and repression. In 1952, Kısakürek was sent to prison accused of the attempted murder of the journalist Ahmet Emin Yalman. His journal was conducting strong and aggressive criticism against Yalman for his "communist sympathies and for being a '*dönme*' or 'secret Jew',"[65] regarding him as enemy of the Turkish nation and Islam. After one and a half years of imprisonment Kısakürek was freed, though he continued being targeted because of his writings and publishing.

After 1960, Kısakürek supported the Justice Party (*Adalet Partisi*) of Süleyman Demirel, while from 1970, the year of establishment of the National Order Party (*Milli Nizam Partisi*) by Necmettin Erbakan, he stood in favor of this Islamic-oriented political party. This lasted at least during the first years of its polit-ical activity, until—as its seems—he was disappointed by the participation of Erbakan in the coalition government (as partner of the Republican People's Party of Bülent Ecevit) in 1974, considering that Erbakan compromised and collab-orated with the Kemalist status quo. In the elections of 1977, Kısakürek stood by the nationalists, namely the Nationalist Movement Party (*Milliyetçi Hareket Partisi*) of Alparslan Türkeş, as well as by nationalist student organizations, "in hopes of forming a religious-nationalist coalition."[66]

The amalgam of Islamism and Turkism should not surprise us or be consid-ered as paradoxical. The (foremost) Islamist Kısakürek was not against Turkish nationalism; as Guida notes, Kısakürek "advocated the inseparable link between Muslim identity and Turkish national identity."[67] Even though he expressed the Islamic and Islamist view of the world's dichotomy in Muslims and non-Muslims, he attributed a leading role to the Turkish nation within the Muslim world. He had the conviction that Islam was the only way to salvation for the Turkish na-tion; the way which Turks have the duty to follow not only in order to save them-selves but also in order to save the world of the East (that is, the Muslim world) and, then, the whole of humanity.[68]

---

64 Thierry Zarcone points out that "in general, Menderes, who is aware of the popularity of his magazine, tries to make it an ally, and goes so far as to support it financially." Thierry Zarcone, *La Turquie moderne*, 179.

65 Michelangelo Guida, "Founders of Islamism", 117.

66 Ibid., 118.

67 Ibid., 119.

68 Necip Fazıl Kısakürek, *İdeolocya Örgüsü*, 21st ed. (Istanbul: Büyük Doğu Yayınları, 2014), 92. *İdeolocya Örgüsü* can be translated as *Ideology Plexus*.

Kısakürek's Thought

In Necip Fazıl's school and university years, we can detect the foundations of his thought and worldview. Western Philosophy (both ancient and contemporary) was not at all unknown to him; in fact, it is known that his thought and literary work was influenced by the philosophical movements of idealism[69] and spiritualism.[70]

Due to his poetry, he is considered a "pioneer of the so-called modern mysticism" in Turkish poetry, as "in the poems of the first period are observed many elements of style of dervish poetry as well as of French poetry with special reference to Baudelaire."[71]

To a significant degree, Kısakürek was influenced by Plato and the French philosophers Henri-Louis Bergson[72] and Maurice Blondel.[73] Plato's Republic,

---

69 "Idealism, in its philosophical sense, is the view that mind and spiritual values are fundamental in the world as a whole. Thus, idealism is opposed to naturalism, that is, to the view that mind and spiritual values have emerged from or are reducible to material things and processes. Philosophical idealism is also opposed to realism and is thus the denial of the common-sense realist view that material things exist independently of being perceived." The Encyclopedia of Philosophy, vol. 4, reprint ed. (New York: Macmillan, 1972), s.v. 'idealism', 110.

70 Spiritualism (or immaterialism) "is the perception that matter is nonexistent. According to spiritualism, reality in its essence is spiritual. According to spiritualism, everything that is considered to be a material thing is nothing more than a bundle of ideas which consist contents of our experience and thus have spiritual character." Philosophy Lexicon [in Greek], new enriched ed. (Athens: Pedio, 2013), 83.

71 Aristotelis Mitraras, Anthology of New Turkish Literature: Poetry [in Greek] (Athens: Papazisis, 2015), 67.

72 Bergson, Henri-Louis (1859–1941): French philosopher, born in Paris of Anglo-Polish parentage, who taught at the Gollège de France in Paris and won the Nobel Prize for Literature in 1927. Bergson is known "for two main doctrines, those of duration and the élan vital. (. . .) Duration is time as experienced by consciousness, and perhaps Bergson's most important insight is that we do not experience the world moment by moment but in a fashion essentially continuous (. . .). Past, present, and future cannot be so separated that it becomes impossible for us to know of the past because only the present is ever present to experience. (. . .) His book Creative Evolution, introducing the élan vital as a sort of life force, probably owed its popularity partly to his attempt, backed by scientific as well as philosophical arguments, to develop a non-Darwinian evolutionism that made room for religion, albeit not for orthodox Christianity." The Oxford Companion to Philosophy (Oxford: Oxford University Press, 1995), 88–89. See also The Encyclopedia of Philosophy, vol. 1, reprint ed., 287–95.

73 Blondel, Maurice (1861–1949): "He is considered one of the foremost French Catholic philosophers of the twentieth century. (. . .) An extended statement of Blondel's

which deals with the ideal city and its organization, the philosophers as ideal rulers, and the forms of government, seems to have to an appreciable extent defined Kısakürek's ideological and political thought and Islamic political vision. From Bergson, he "used the definitions of nationalism and spiritualism-mysticism," observes Duran, while the influence of Blondel's philosophy of action is apparent in the special importance that Kısakürek attributed to the notion of action.[74] As Duran adds, Kısakürek once talked about "resemblance between himself who revived Islam and Blondel who revived French Catholicism"; moreover, he considered Islam as "an unending action," and God as "the absolute actioner."[75]

This philosophical and intellectual base is strongly characterized by religion (Islam) and (Islamic) mysticism, symbolism,[76] and existentialism.[77] It offers a set of ideas and elements that can be used as a response to contemporaneous materialism and positivism. This does not mean, however, that these were the only philosophical elements of Kısakürek's thought and spirit.

Philosophical currents and the intellectual elite of Western Europe in the nineteenth and the beginning of the twentieth century contributed to the forging

---

philosophy in found in the book L' Action, first published in 1893 (...). The claim of Blondel's early work is that philosophy must take its impetus from action rather than from pure thought. The expression "action" is used in a wide sense to refer to the whole of our life, thinking, feeling, willing. (...) It is indeed this experience itself that motivates the philosophical quest, for man by his nature must act, and then he cannot help questioning the menaing of his action. (...) Since action is concrete, the beliefs that arise out of action and the experience of acting are not abstract formulations. It is in action that we apprehend God (...)." *The Encyclopedia of Philosophy*, vol. 1, reprint ed., 323–24.

74 Burhanettin Duran, *Transformation of Islamist political thought*, 302.
75 Ibid., footnote 129.
76 Symbolism: "The manifestation or expression of of ideas, not in a direct and explicit manner, but indirectly, though symbols. Symbolism was mainly used in religion and art." *Philosophy Lexicon* [in Greek], 578.
77 Existentialism: "According to the teachings of existentialism, it is of prior importance for us to turn ourselves directly and exclusively to our own nature in order to understand it (...) There are two main types of existentialism: atheist existentialism and religious existentialism." Philosophy Lexicon [in Greek], 641. "Existentialism may perhaps be considered most fruitfully as a historical movement in which connections of dependence and influence can be traced from one writer to another. (...) The key themes are the individual and systems; intentionality; being and absurdity; the nature and significance of choice; the role of extreme experiences; and the nature of communication." *The Encyclopedia of Philosophy*, vol. 3, reprint ed., 147.

of Kısakürek's thought and reflection—mainly during his youth. However, we should not neglect the fact that the influence of Islam is strong in his work. The influence of Ibn Khaldun[78] is obvious in Kısakürek's perception of history and the historical course of people and empires, where the idea of circularity is dominant; that is, the idea that societies and empires rise, prosper, decline, and fall, and this happens in successive circles in history. Through this theorization of history and the course of human civilization, Kısakürek conceived the history of Islam and Islamic world, as well as the history of Turkish people (pre-Islamic, pre-Ottoman, Ottoman, and citizens of the Republic of Turkey) as an expression of a circular course, which deterministically will be put, again, on a growth path.

Kısakürek considered al-Ghazali[79] to be one of the greatest spiritualists[80] and stood to reason to be influenced by his work, ideas, and the relationship of al-Ghazali with mysticism. Elements of al-Farabi's[81] thinking are also evident in the political thought of Kısakürek, and can probably be seen as another channel (in addition to European philosophers) through which the notions and concepts of Plato's philosophical thought were transferred to Necip Fazıl. This contributed to the formation of Kısakürek's platonic tendencies, such as, for example, his beliefs about the organization and administration of the ideal state, the relation between politics and religion, and the prominent role of philosophers in political leadership.

---

78 Ibn Khaldun (Tunis, 1332–Cairo, 1406): Great Arab historian, famous for his "Prolegomena" ("Muqadimmah"), that is, the introduction to the world history that he wrote; a unique and pioneering spirit that is recognized as having written philosophy of history, and having contributed to history, sociology, political science, political economy, anthropology, and other disciplines.

79 Al-Ghazali (1058–1111): Prominent jurist, theologian, mystic, and philosopher who lived in various parts of the Muslim world (Tus, Nishapur, Baghdat, Syria, Palestine, and elsewhere); he criticized earlier philosophers and the Aristotelian logic, and highlighted the importance of religion, God, Islamic mysticism, and mystical experience in the human effort to understand the world.

80 As Duran notes, Kısakürek mentioned "in one occasion the names of Socrates, Plato, al-Ghazali, Pascal, Bergson, and Blondel as the greatest spiritualists." Burhanettin Duran, *Transformation of Islamist political thought*, 302, footnote 127.

81 Al-Farabi (ca. 870–ca. 950): Prominent philosopher and scientist, who was known in the Muslim world as the "second master" behind Aristotle. He was highly knowledgeable about the philosophy of Plato, Aristotle and Neoplatonism; his works have contributed to the fields of logic, political philosophy, practical philosophy, philosophy of religion, as well as mathematics and music.

His teachers and professors in Istanbul played an important role in the formulation of Kısakürek's religious conscience and Islamist thought, but even more important was the role of his mystic *sheikh* (master), Abdulhakim Arvasi.[82] Kısakürek first met Arvasi at the age of 30 (in 1934) and his intellectual, moral, and ideological effect was the catalyst for the later thinking and action of the young poet and writer. The importance of this relationship is confirmed by the fact that Kısakürek renounced his writings and poems dated before 1934 on the grounds that they were contrary to Islamic law.[83]

According to his own words, "his political and intellectual life could be classified into two periods: old Kısakürek before his meeting with Abdulhakim Arvasi, and new Kısakürek after this meeting."[84] As Duran further writes, "Through this meeting the bohemian and crisis-ridden life of a republican poet was transformed into an Islamist intellectual who ideologized Islam as an alternative ideology to both western political ideologies of capitalism and communism and to the Kemalist ideology and who shouldered an ideal of reestablishing the Turkish state and society on the basis of Islamic principles."[85]

In a similar way, Yavuz observes the following: "In the 1940s and 1950s, he was the first Turkish Muslim intellectual to frame Islam as a holistic and totalist ideology, known as *Büyük Doğu* (Great Orient). The process of ideologization of Islam was carried out in "opposition" to the Kemalist project of Westernization."[86] In other words, the ideological Islamic program of Kısakürek was created in the search for opposition and criticism to the reformation and modernization program from above during the first decades of the Turkish Republic. Obviously, the anti-Kemalist critique expressed by Kısakürek and his journal was manifested through many forms: as antisemitic and anti-masonic, anti-materialist, anti-positivist, anti-utilitarian, anti-capitalist, etc.[87]

According to Cemil Aydın, who considers Kısakürek to be one of the leading Islamists of the first decades of the Turkish Republic and includes him in the

82 Abdulhakim Arvasi (Van province, 1865–Ankara, 1943): Islamic scholar and spiritual leader of the Nakshibendi mystical Islamic order, who lived and taught mainly in Van and Istanbul. The Büyük Doğu Publishing house of the Kısakürek family has published some of his works.
83 Burhanettin Duran, *Transformation of Islamist political thought*, 206, footnote 87.
84 Ibid., 206.
85 Ibid.
86 M. Hakan Yavuz, *Islamic Political Identity*, 116.
87 Levent Cantek, "Büyük Doğu", in *Muhafazakârlık*, ed. Ahmet Çiğdem, vol. 5 of Modern Türkiye'de Siyasi Düşünce (Istanbul: İletişim Yayınları, 2003), 654.

wider group of the Islamist-nationalist intelligentsia, Kısakürek "published his *Büyük Doğu* (The Great East) in 1943 to disseminate an Islamist-nationalist ideology that was almost the opposite of everything Kemalism represented."[88] Aydın places Kısakürek's thought into a wider thinking frame of Occidentalism and essentialism, underlining the following:

> The new conservatism and nationalism of Islamist critiques of the West, symbolized by Kısakürek's writings, strengthened the occidentalist essentialism about the decadent, materialist, positivist, soulless, immoral, communist, individualistic, and 'Masonic' West. Kısakürek and other Islamists also used this occidentalist rhetoric strategically to weaken the legitimacy of the Kemalist regime itself.[89]

This important turning point in the life and spiritual growth of Kısakürek brings into focus the importance of Islamic (and, in particular, Nakshibendi) mysticism for the Islamist movement and thought in Turkey.[90] In the light of Kısakürek's case, the decisive influence of Islamic mystical orders to both intellectuals and politicians of contemporary Turkey should be underlined.

Büyük Doğu

Büyük Doğu (Great East) is the major ideological and theoretical work of Kısakürek's political (Islamist) vision. In his own words, *Büyük Doğu* is a "creation of concrete faith, vision, and measurement."[91] It is described by Kısakürek in the following way:

> The East, which is embraced and unified by the Great East, is related to no racial or geographic plan outside the country's frontiers. (...) We seek the Great East in a plan of spirit and elements that is comprised in today's and tomorrow's frontiers of our country. This is aimed to be realized not inside its own space frame, but in a time frame...[92]

Necip Fazıl further explains the causes and goals of this pursuit:

> The fake revolutions that continue since the *Tanzimat*, as well as the fake heroes these revolutions have constructed, are in practice the main issue of our struggle. What we lost in our own selves and our own pockets, what we gropingly searched [to find] upon

---

88 Cemil Aydın, "Between Occidentalism and the Global Left: Islamist Critiques of the West in Turkey," *Comparative Studies of South Asia, Africa and the Middle East*, 26:3 (2006): 453.

89 Ibid.

90 For more about Turkish Nakshibendi Islam and its political dimensions, see M. Hakan Yavuz, *Islamic Political identity*, 133–50.

91 Necip Fazıl Kısakürek, *İdeolocya Örgüsü*, 9.

92 Ibid., 10.

like blind men outside of us and in foreign pockets, skimming over things and events, losing more than actually finding, thinking of finding but actually losing more, like the key we lost in the sand and while searching we dug a hole [in the sand] deeper and deeper... This is the Great East. This is a name of sense, of substance, of time and space and, namely [this] is [a] symbol of the universe of the East that a great spirit will offer as exemplar to the whole humanity.[93]

For Kısakürek "the real Islam and its fundamental values prescribed as Sharia must form the basis of the state and society in the worldview of Great East."[94] He regarded Islamic law (*sharia*) as a whole of principles, as well as a "divine institution."[95] He also noted that "prosperity for the Muslim world will only be achieved when the truly and deeply Muslims turn both to the evident and the mystical [element]."[96] In other words, when they turn simultaneously to the sharia, that is, the evident, exterior element of Islam, and to mysticism, the mystical, interior element of Islam.

The Great East, as both a political vision and a plan, concentrates all the principles and virtues of the theoretical ideal state of Kısakürek. The Great East is established on nine ideological principles: spiritualism, qualitativism, personalism, moralism, nationalism, regulation of capital and property, communitarianism,[97] orderliness (and order), and interventionism.[98] These principles disclose the fully-developed philosophical background of Kısakürek's thought, as well as the great importance he attributed to spiritualism—and, thus, to Islamic mysticism.

More specifically, Kısakürek describes the organs and the administration structures[99] of the ideal state (of the Great East), which he calls *Başyüce Devlet* or *Başyücelik Devleti* (highest or supreme state). At the head of the state there is a prominent leader, the supreme ruler (*Başyüce*), while the state's institutional organization comprises the supreme assembly (*Yüceler Kurultayı*), supreme

---

93 Ibid., 12.

94 Burhanettin Duran, *Transformation of Islamist political thought*, 296.

95 Ibid.

96 Necip Fazıl Kısakürek, *İdeolocya Örgüsü*, 190–91.

97 The word used by Kısakürek is "cemiyetçilik"; it can be understood as "communitarianism," though it might also be used as "sociologism" in Turkish.

98 In Turkish: ruhçuluk, keyfiyetçilik, şahsiyetçilik, ahlakçılık, milliyetçilik, sermaye ve mülkiyette tedbircilik, cemiyetçilik, nizamcılık, müdahalecilik. Kısakürek explains each one of these principles in his *İdeolocya Örgüsü*, 389–410. The term "keyfiyetçilik" could also be translated as "circumstantialism"; I owe this note to Zuhal Mert Uzuner, Associate Professor of International Relations at Marmara University, in Istanbul.

99 Necip Fazıl Kısakürek, *İdeolocya Örgüsü*, 285–309.

government (*Başyücelik Hükûmeti*), supreme religious authority (*Yüce Din Dairesi*), people's council (*Halk Divanı*), and supreme academy (*Başyücelik Akademyası*).

The supreme ruler of the state excels in ethics, knowledge, and intelligence, and is elected by the supreme assembly for five years. The supreme assembly is, in fact, an assembly of intellectuals, an assembly in which the members are characterized by high knowledge, ethics, and faith in God and Islamic law. Therefore, it would be an assembly which expresses the will of God. The supreme government is the governing council, consisting of the supreme ruler and eleven member-ministers. Each of the eleven ministries has three deputy ministries. The supreme religious authority is determined by the supreme ruler and deals with Islamic education, religious institutions, and religious matters. The people's council is convened each year and gives the opportunity for the people to communicate with the leadership. The supreme academy has the duty to educate and edify the people, and to teach what is good, right, and beautiful to the people. There are three sections: theory and mind, science and discovery, and literature and fine arts.

For Kısakürek, the ideal state that will emanate from the Islamic revolution must follow the principles of Islam, Islamic law, and Islamic mysticism. This is what matters and not whether the regime will be a democracy, an oligarchy, or a monarchy.[100] The supreme assembly, being an assembly of the intellectuals,[101] must obey the truth of God, and obey the phrase "Sovereignty belongs to God."[102] The Great East, underlines Thierry Zarcone, "is the first work from the very beginning of the republican period that considers Islam to be a social, cultural, and political system. For Fazıl, state sovereignty is not founded on the people, as the main democratic principle insist upon, but on God."[103]

Kısakürek's ideal state is a state of centered, totalitarian, and authoritarian governance; as Duran notes "one may find many similarities between Kısakürek's idealization of state and society in *İdeolocya Örgüsü* (ideological web) and Plato's ideal state in the 'Republic'," adding that "Kısakürek's *başyücelik devleti* bore marks of both juristic theory of caliphate and al-Farabi's ideal city."[104]

---

100 Ibid., 223.
101 In Türkish: "münevverler".
102 Necip Fazıl Kısakürek, *İdeolocya Örgüsü*, 225.
103 Thierry Zarcone, *La Turquie moderne*, 179.
104 Burhanettin Duran, *Transformation of Islamist political thought*, 306.

Another important element of Kısakürek's political thought is the idea of revolution (*inkılâp*) itself. Kısakürek had faith in the revolution that was destined to break out, underlining that "since the era of Suleiman the Magnificent we are expecting the real revolution,"[105] while he explained: "Since 400 years we are waiting for a revolution and a revolutionary. Are we now in 1973? We are waiting for that since 1566 exactly."[106]

The idea of revolution is not something foreign to the political and social circumstances and the ideological movements of the time, both in domestic and international politics, and shows the idealization of revolutions as the only possible way to achieve radical political change and the overthrow of the old regime. The revolution of the Bolsheviks, as well as the revolution of the Young Turks, occurred during the first decades of the twentieth century, while there was also the so-called "revolution" (or "revolutionary reforms") of Mustafa Kemal (Atatürk). The reference to an Islamic revolution can be considered as an important contribution of Kısakürek to later Islamic thought and political theory.

The revolutionary Islamic spirit of the Great East inspired a group of radical Islamists that originated from the party organizations of Erbakan's political Islam, which during the 1980s formed the extremist Islamist organization *İslami Büyük Doğu Akıncılar-Cephesi* - İBDA-C (Front of Fighters of the Islamic Great East). With cells in Turkey and cities in Western Europe, İBDA-C developed lethal extremist action in Turkey during the 1990s and the early 2000s.[107]

Even more, Kısakürek's political thought influenced, to varying extents, almost all of the conservative (Islamist, nationalist, right-wing) politicians, parties, and organizations in Turkey after the middle of the 20th century. It can be noted here that the ideological program and vision of Erbakan's *Milli Görüş* (National View) in the 1970s and afterwards presents elements of the Great East. Furthermore, political representatives and even leading figures of the Justice and Development Party (JDP) do not hide their preference for the ideas and spirit of Kısakürek. It is known that Abdullah Gül, a founding member of JDP, who has served as Prime Minister, Foreign Affairs Minister, and President of the Turkish Republic, was in his youth inspired by the ideas and personality of Kısakürek, and was a leading member in the National Turkish Students' Union (*Milli Türk Talebe Birliği* / MTTB), a student organization inspired to a large

---

105 Necip Fazıl Kısakürek, *İdeolocya Örgüsü*, 161.
106 Ibid., 163.
107 See Konstantinos Gogos, *Turkish Political Islam and Islamist Networks in Germany* [in Greek] (Athens: Livanis, 2011), 160–63.

degree by Kısakürek's ideas. Turkish President Recep Tayyip Erdoğan was also a member of the MTTB in his youth,[108] and as a matter of fact has used in his political speeches lines from Kısakürek, as in the case of a party gathering of the JDP, in November 2012, when he stated: "Tomorrow is certainly ours, and it naturally belongs to us. A day rises, a day sets, the everlasting future is ours."[109]

In Turkey, especially in recent years which have been marked by the hegemony of political Islam and the flowering of Islamic associations and organizations, the work and thought of Kısakürek have experienced a strong surge in popularity and have been a major subject of study. Indeed, scholar and writer Mustafa Miyasoğlu[110] wrote regarding Kısakürek's intellectual work and heritage:

> In Turkey today, right-wing, left-wing, even Kemalists study Necip Fazıl's views. (...) Those who study history, religion, philosophy, Sufism, theatre and poetry are confronted with Necip Fazıl's views and works. Whoever contemporary writer, intellectual, poet, writer, philosopher, even theologian doesn't know Necip Fazıl is not considered serious. [Necip Fazıl] has become so very important, so cult, so very accepted. Necip Fazıl is an important genius that was created in the twentieth century by the Turkish nation and has given one very important message to the humanity. This genius has a global range.[111]

Moreover, Miyasoğlu supported the idea that the "Arab Spring" in Egypt was inspired by the Great East:

> The "Greater Middle East Project" of America went bankrupt, but the "Great East" of Necip Fazıl is still [included] in the agenda. The Arab Spring, which commenced from Egypt, was realized thanks to the intellectuals that were influenced by Necip Fazıl. Egyptian Professor Dr. Muhammed Harb, who is really popular in the Islamic world, is one of those intellectuals. Muhammed Harb was weaned on Necip Fazıl's works, he did in Turkey his Ph.D. thesis on History. Harb, his students and his friends sparked the Arab Spring. The inspiration of the Arab Spring is found in Necip Fazıl's works.[112]

These words, excessive or not, reveal the way some Muslim intellectuals and writers conceive of Kısakürek's thought and the influence he continues to exercise.

---

108 Michelangelo Guida, "Founders of Islamism", 111.

109 Ayşe Hür, "Necip Fazıl Kısakürek'in 'Öteki' Portresi", *Radikal*, January 6, 2013, http://www.radikal.com.tr/yazarlar/ayse-hur/necip-fazil-kisakurekin-oteki-portresi-1115579/ (accessed December 28, 2013).

110 Mustafa Miyasoğlu (1946–2013): Turkish literature scholar, poet and author of literature essays and biographies, with expertise in the work of Kısakürek.

111 "Türk Edebiyatının Çok Yönlü Şahsiyeti: Necip Fazıl", *Akşam*, May 24, 2012, https://www.aksam.com.tr/kultur-sanat/turk-edebiyatinin-cok-yonlu-sahsiyeti-necip-fazil-117635h/haber-117635 (accessed November 8, 2015).

112 Ibid.

Muhammed Harb, an Egyptian professor of Ottoman History,[113] has translated works of Necip Fazıl into Arabic and speaks with enthusiasm of Kısakürek and his thought, highlighting, in fact, that he considers "*İdeolocya Örgüsü* the most important book of his reflection on the Eastern world... It's a wonder that this book has not until now been translated in all languages of the world."[114]

The Role of Intellectuals

Kısakürek envisions and pursues one highly important role for the intellectuals. He considers that (Muslim) intellectuals must take the lead of the Islamic state and guide Islamic society—this is a fundamental and characteristic feature of his reflection. Kısakürek's intellectual is a thinker and also a hero, has his own worldview, and can lead society to salvation. In his view, throughout history "Intellectuals as the avant-garde had been always in a position to revolt in their search for the ideal society and state."[115] In the Ottoman Empire since the period of the *Tanzimat* reforms "false intellectuals/heroes who exploited the national will of the enemies of the nation and of Islam" had prevailed.[116] Furthermore he strongly criticized important (Kemalist) intellectuals of the Turkish Republic.[117]

According to Kısakürek, in Turkish history during the last century, the type of thinker-philosopher that could reinterpret and spread the spirit and ideology of Islam did not exist;[118] in fact, as Duran notes, "in Kısakürek's mind, the thinker who Turks needed was a combination of thinker and statesman, a kind of Platonian philosopher-king."[119] The intellectual (of Kısakürek) has "the vanguard role in the revolution, putting the ideology into action" and "becomes the expected saver of Turkey and the Islamic world."[120]

During the last years of his life, in the context of the 1980 military coup, Kısakürek supported the intervention of the army and set as a primary goal the

---

113 Professor at the Istanbul Sabahattin Zaim University.
114 See his interview in "Ya Rab! Canımı İstanbul'da al!", *Yeni Akit,* October 5, 2014, https://www.yeniakit.com.tr/haber/ya-rab-canimi-istanbulda-al-32217.html (accessed February 10, 2016).
115 Burhanettin Duran, *Transformation of Islamist political thought,* 212–13.
116 Ibid., 213. Kısakürek mentions the names Mustafa Reşit Paşa, Fuat Paşa, Ali Paşa, Namık Kemal, Ziya Gökalp.
117 Such as Nazım Hikmet, Peyami Safa, or the Kadro movement. See Burhanettin Duran, *Transformation of Islamist political thought,* 214.
118 Ibid., 221.
119 Ibid., footnote 3.
120 Ibid., 214.

salvation of the nation and the country. For obtaining this objective, he proposed specific measures to the military—in line with his own conservative and Islamist ideological framework. Among the measures he proposed was the establishment of an "assembly of intellectuals" which would take the lead in governance decisions, as well as the establishment of an "academy of intellectuals" which would take decisions and initiatives in the fields of language, alphabet, and culture.[121]

Views on Turkish History and Islam

Kısakürek does not miss a chance to underline and glorify the leading role of the Turks and the Ottomans in the history of Islam and of Islamic empires, seeking not only the reinforcement of Islamic identity and the awareness of the Turkish citizen, but also the disintegration of the Kemalist view and propaganda of history. According to Cemil Aydın's assessment, it is particularly important that "Kısakürek helped create an anti-official history narrative by calling the entire tradition of Ottoman reform and Kemalism (except the period of Abdülhamid II) a betrayal of the national and Islamic self by a collaborating, sell-out elite."[122]

Moreover, Kısakürek believed that, since Islam has fallen in Turkey,[123] it can only rise again from Turkey and "he observed the Islamic movements in the Arab world and the Indian subcontinent with suspicion and detachment."[124]

Text: "Our Crisis"

The text entitled *"Bizde Buhran"* (Our Crisis) is highly enlightening when it comes to Kısakürek's view of history—and is indicative of his literary talent. An excerpt follows:

> Our crisis consists of two long periods: the pre-*Tanzimat* and the post-*Tanzimat* period.
> The first of these two periods lasted more than three centuries before the *Tanzimat*.
> Each of these two long periods can be divided into three different parts. The three phases of the first period are [the following]: from Suleiman the Magnificent to Mehmet IV, from Mehmet IV to Selim III, from Selim III to Abdulmejid... While the three phases of the second period are from the *Tanzimat* until the *Meşrutiyet*, from the *Meşrutiyet* until the Republic and from the Republic until today...

---

121 Ibid., 293.
122 Cemil Aydın, "Between Occidentalism and the Global Left", 453.
123 Meaning the establishment of the Turkish Republic and the abolition of the caliphate and the Ottoman Islamic institutions.
124 Cemil Aydın, "Between Occidentalism and the Global Left," 453.

If we desire to express in centuries the duration of the each period's phase, then we are talking about a span of our centuries that begins in the middle of the sixteenth century and ends in the middle of the twentieth: in the end of the sixteenth century the disease creates the first bridgehead under our skin, in the end of the seventeenth century it starts to pass on the skin, in the eighteenth century [the disease] is fully settled and in the twentieth century this chronic disease shows that its settlement was structured around fake medicine for cure.

In the first long period of our crisis, our main disease was rough and crude backwardness... In the second long period, our dead-drunkenness was the amazement, the confusion, and the lack of [our own] personality...

(...) One period had religious fanatics, the other one had atheist fanatics, rough and crude followers... Whatever has fallen on our heads has come from them.[125]

In another text Kısakürek briefly points out that the period of Islam's (and also of the Turks') decline can be seen and understood in four phases:[126] from Suleiman the Magnificent to the *Tanzimat*, from the *Tanzimat* to the *Meşrutiyet*,[127] from the *Meşrutiyet* to the Republic, and from the Republic up to the present day.[128]

Text: "Line for Historical Periodization"[129]

It is of particular interest the way Kısakürek sees the history of the Turks, and Islam's position in it, from the ancient pre-Islamic times until the Turkish Republic. Indicative of this viewpoint is the text entitled "Line for Historical Periodization", an extract from which is cited here:

Let us leave apart the mythological atmosphere that covers much earlier centuries; we have documented that in the first, in the second, in the third, in the fourth, in the fifth and in the sixth centuries the entire essence of the Turkish world, like a whirlwind, like a torrent, a lightning, a thunder, [this essence] was made up by a unique insubmissive enlivening force which had not yet been crystallized, had not found shape, had not reached the expression of a composed cultural context. And this unique force of life continued to flow for centuries, [and was] attached to the front of the horse's thighs that put fire in their mane, longing for the great architecture of faith that would match this far-reaching structure with its spirit.

---

125 See Necip Fazıl Kısakürek, *İdeolocya Örgüsü*, 54–55.

126 Entitled "How was Islam destroyed?" (*İslam nasıl bozuldu?*); to be found in Necip Fazıl Kısakürek, *İdeolocya Örgüsü*, 146–56.

127 The years of Ottoman constitutional monarchy, between December 1876 and February 1878.

128 In this case, the year 1948.

129 In Turkish: *Fasledici Tarih Çizgisi*.

In the seventh and eighth centuries, the Turkish world, partially and gradually, accepted the Islamic religion and linked its spirit to it by sword, in the most gentle fulfillment of its delivery to [it] and in front of the majestic purity of the divine construction.

In the ninth, tenth, eleventh, and twelfth centuries, the Turkish world, again partially and gradually, began to create the first protoplasms of the brightest civilization, emitting from the exceptionally faithful and unique crystal of its spirit and temperament, the lights of the intellectual content it had acquired.

The terms of an actual global civilization related to the state and society, creation and progress, justice and the politics that exist [in our civilization] are found in the time of the establishment of the Ottomans: in the thirteenth century...

The fourteenth century, in spite of the divisions provoked by certain causes due to the leadership, was our era of ecstasy, love, order, movement, and offense. This movement and offense has the shape of a confrontation between two opposed cultural worlds and flows to the West.

In the fifteenth century and in the same ecstasy, love, and order, our movement wore the crown of a great victory and reached a point where it created in the Western world a new phase.

We reached the climax of our rise in the sixteenth century, in which we set up the greatest empire in history, but again we deviated to arrogance and insensibility, we couldn't notice the ferment of the Western world that was being born, while the ecstasy and our love started to freeze (...)[130]

It is worth here adding the note of Thierry Zarcone on how Kısakürek perceives the history of Turkish Islam:

He compares the five main periods of this history to roads. The first period, that extends from the foundation of the Empire to Suleiman the Magnificent, is an asphalted road; the second that goes from this great sultan's period to the time of the *Tanzimat* reforms is a road covered with mud; the third, that goes until the Young Turk revolution, is a road full of rockeries and brush; the fourth, that goes until the Republic, is a road for goats; finally, the one that goes through the Republic to our days is a road for moles.[131]

According to Zarcone, the fact that Kısakürek regards all the reformers of the *Tanzimat* era, the Young Ottomans, and the Young Turks, as "fake heroes" should hardly surprise.[132] Nevertheless, it must be mentioned that within this course of decline and destruction, Kısakurek believed that Sultan Abdul Hamid II stood out for his leadership and politics, as his objective was—according to Kısakürek—to maintain the empire's unity and to combine the principles of

---

130 Necip Fazıl Kısakürek, *İdeolocya Örgüsü*, 143–45.
131 Thierry Zarcone, *La Turquie moderne*, 179.
132 Ibid., 179–80.

Islam with technical progress. In addition, Kısakürek believed that Sultan Abdul Hamid II was inspired by and followed the main ideals of the Great East.[133]

For Kısakürek, neither the leading figures of the Tanzimat, nor the Young Turks and, later, Mustafa Kemal, were real modernists or reformers. However, Abdul Hamid II was a modernist because he combined the spirit of Islam and the East with the materialism and technology of the West.

The Relation between Islam and the Military

As has already been pointed out in previous pages, Kısakürek's support for the military regime in 1980, as well as his distaste for democracy and secularism in Turkey—at least in the form they had been implemented up until then—were particularly evident. Nonetheless, even before 1980, the value Kısakürek gives to the role of the army is important and evident in his work.

Necip Fazıl recognizes the special mission of the Turkish army to achieve the ideals of the Great East, and the diffusion of ethos and religion of the authentic Islam as he envisioned. He expresses a militaristic spirit which he aims to explain and define; according to Kısakürek "the ideal of the Great East is militaristic."[134] Nevertheless, "this militarism is not based on arms, material power and material resources, [this militarism] is not boorish and foolish, neither expresses violence and aggressiveness, as once happened in the corps of the Janissaries. The ideal of the Great East is opposed to that to the very highest degree..."[135] However, he notes that: "The army does not exist for the army; the army exists for the nation."[136] He likens the army to the "fist of the Muslim community,"[137] while he has also written that "Islam holds really tight the army and the soldiers."[138]

Apparently, it is an army gripped by the ideal of the Great East; an army that will serve its purpose, and will be gripped by the spirit of the Turkish Golden Horde, which is for the contemporary Turks—as Kısakürek believes—a shining example of harmony and complementarity between the head and the fist, that is, between nation and armed forces.[139]

---

133 See Burhanettin Duran, *Transformation of Islamist political thought*, 230.
134 Necip Fazıl Kısakürek, *İdeolocya Örgüsü*, 272.
135 Ibid.
136 Ibid., 273.
137 Ibid.
138 Ibid., 130.
139 Ibid., 274.

Conclusion

The ideas and activities of Necip Fazıl Kısakürek show that he combines and represents many elements and tendencies of the Islamist movement in a rare and fertile synthesis. His Islamist thought has cultural and political dimensions, which is also accompanied—in practice—by political actions and participation. His Islamist thought also has strong nationalist, militaristic, mystical, and revolutionary dimensions.

His vision for the Great East, an Islamic Great East, became the object of description and analysis in his book entitled *Ideology Plexus*, which is of considerable value as a text of Islamic political ideology and philosophy. In the Islamist thought of Kısakürek, the dichotomy between East and West is predominant, and the antithesis between East and West is existent and strong in Kısakürek's thought, accompanied by his faith in the supremacy of the East and Islam, as well as in the prominent role of the Turks. The Great East of Kısakürek includes and is defined by Islam and Turkish identity.

Kısakürek has strongly influenced and continues to influence intellectuals, writers, politicians, and religious groups in Turkey. His ideological and theoretical influence on the parties of political Islam in Turkey, and on leading political personalities (such as Recep Tayyip Erdoğan) is obvious and important. In the field of literary production, his impact is evident in the subsequent generations of Islamist writers and intellectuals.

Moreover, it should be said that Kısakürek's ideas and thought act as a bridge and a link between the Islamist thought of the last decades of the Ottoman Empire and the Islamist intellectuals of recent decades in Turkey. His thought and writings may also have had an impact outside Turkey's frontiers; however, this is something one should investigate thoroughly before drawing conclusions.

During the final period of his life (namely the years of the military-led government from 1980–1983) Necip Fazıl received special honors and awards for his literary work, poetry, and ideas.[140] In 2014, the newspaper *Star* established the "Necip Fazıl Prizes" (*Necip Fazıl Ödülleri*) which are given annually by a selection committee to writers, essayists, poets, and scholars who are recognized to have made important contributions to Turkish literature, culture, and history.

---

140 The Turkish Literature Foundation honored and characterized him as "the sultan of poets" in 1980; he was given the Great Prize of the Ministry of Culture in 1980; he was honored by the Turkish Writers Union in 1982. See "Türk Edebiyatının Çok Yönlü Şahsiyeti: Necip Fazıl."

The study of Kısakürek's Islamist thought and theoretical work is growing in today's Turkey, which reveals the importance of his thought and its continuing contribution to the strengthening and formation of both the Islamic identity and the Islamist movement in Turkey.

Chapter 3 Ali Bulaç

Ali Bulaç is a prolific writer, and one of the most well-known and widely read Islamist writers in modern Turkey. Of the three writers that this book deals with, Bulaç has attracted the most research attention even outside Turkey—without this meaning that too many studies have been published on his views and writings.[141] As far as the Greek bibliography is concerned, the first reference to Bulaç—and to modern Turkish Islamist intellectuals—was made by Ioannis Mazis,[142] followed later by two of my own articles.[143]

This chapter aims to offer a representative picture of Bulaç's Islamist thought. It intends to present the main characteristics of his thinking and argumentation, and to reveal his views and ideas with regard to questions related to politics and government, contemporary Turkey, the West, and Islam.

---

141 Michael Meeker was one of the first Western scholars who dealt with the ideas and writings of Bulaç and other Islamist intellectuals, and wrote an enlightening text under the title "The New Muslim Intellectuals in the Republic of Turkey," published in 1991. Anat Lapidot in her unpublished PhD dissertation devoted one chapter to Bulaç's Islamist thought; see Anat Lapidot, *Islam and Nationalism: A Study of Contemporary Political Thought in Turkey, 1980–1990* (PhD diss., Durham University 1995), 144–75. With regard to Turkish researchers who wrote in a Western language, one should note Nermin Abadan-Unat, "Ideologische Strömungen in der Türkei in den 90er Jahren," *Südosteuropa Mitteilungen* 4 (1997), 291–300; Menderes Çinar and Ayşe Kadioğlu, "An Islamic Critique of Modernity in Turkey: Politics of Difference Backwards," ORIENT 40:1 (1999), 53–69. Among the subsequent publications in Turkish language, see Ferhat Kentel, "1990'ların İslami Düşünce Dergileri ve Yeni Müslüman Entelektüeller," in *İslamcılık*, ed. Yasin Aktay, vol. 6 of Modern Türkiye'de Siyasi Düşünce (Istanbul: İletişim Yayınları, 2004), 721–81.
142 See Ioannis Mazis, *Mystical Islamic Orders and Political-Economic Islam in Modern Turkey* [in Greek] (Athens: Proskinio, 2000), 122–24 and 171–79.
143 See Konstantinos Gogos, "Turkish Islamist Intellectuals and the Islamist movement: The view of Ali Bulaç" [in Greek], in G. Salakidis (ed.), *Tourkologika* (Thessaloniki: Ant. Stamoulis, 2011), 423–36; Konstantinos Gogos, "Contemporary Turkish Islamist Intellectuals and the Rise of Political Islam in Turkey" [in Greek], Γεωστρατηγική [Geostrategy] 9 (May–August 2006): 95–105.

Short Biography

Ali Bulaç was born in 1951 in Mardin, a city in Southern Turkey close to the Syrian border. His family is of Arab origin and Arabic is Bulaç's mother tongue.[144] He completed his secondary education in a public religious school (*Imam Hatip* school) in the same city, while he also attended courses in a clandestine religious seminary (*medrese*) for a number of years.[145] He studied Theology at the Higher Islam Institute (*Yüksek İslam Enstitüsü*) in Istanbul, from which he graduated in 1975. Afterwards, he studied Sociology at the University of Istanbul, from which he graduated in 1980.[146] This intellectual and spiritual background, in combination with his rich publishing activity and published work, make his readers regard him as a sociologist, a theologian, a columnist, a publisher, and an essayist. He is married and father of five children.

Bulaç's Publishing Activities and Writings

Bulaç's publishing and writing activities began in the 1970s.[147] Initially he published texts in the journal *Hareket* (Movement),[148] while in 1976 he founded the publishing house *Düşünce* (Thought) and published a journal by the same name. In 1984, he founded the publication *İnsan* (Human), and during the period 1985–1992 Ali Bulaç was the director of the journal *Kitap Dergisi* (Book's Journal). Soon after, he published the journal *Bilgi ve Hikmet* (Knowledge and

---

144 See Michelangelo Guida, "The New Islamists' Understanding of Democracy in Turkey: The Examples of Ali Bulaç and Hayreddin Karaman," *Turkish Studies* 11:3 (2010): 351; Konstantinos Gogos, "Turkish Islamist Intellectuals": 424–25.

145 As Guida mentions, Bulaç "studied for several years in a clandestine medrese in Mardin, where he learned the pillars of religion and fiqh." Michelangelo Guida, "The New Islamists' Understanding": 351.

146 Ibid. This is something that has led German scholar Günter Seufert to note that Bulaç possesses both "solid theological training" and "a semi-academic university education." See Günter Seufert, "Porträt Ali Bulaç: Jenseits von Konservatismus und Nationalismus," Qantara.de, February 16, 2007, http://de.qantara.de/inhalt/portrat-ali-bulac-jenseits-von-konservatismus-und-nationalismus (accessed May 6, 2016).

147 Very informative about Bulaç's biography and professional career is the article of Michelangelo Guida, "The New Islamists' Understanding": 351–52.

148 The journal *Hareket* was published by Nurettin Topçu (1909–1975), an important intellectual of the Islamist and nationalist movement, whose Islamist stance was more academic and moderate than that of Kısakürek. The journal *Hareket*, published for the first time in 1939, was the first Islamist journal published in Turkey after 1925 and the secularizing, nationalist, and modernizing reforms of the 1920s and 1930s.

Wisdom);[149] it was published for the first time in 1993 but closed down after two years and twelve volumes. As well as Bulaç, many other important Turkish intellectuals wrote in this journal.[150] In 2002—together with Ali Kemal Temizer, Ahmet Ağırakça, Sedat Yenigün, and Selahattin Eş Çakırgil—Bulaç founded the journal *Bilgi ve Düşünce* (Knowledge and Thought).[151]

Bulaç was one of the founding members of the newspaper *Zaman* (Time) in 1986, but he resigned by the end of 1987. According to Michelangelo Guida, Bulaç could not get along with the editor, Mehmet Şevket Eygi, who was appointed by the new board of trustees which was very close to, at that time, the emerging Fethullah Gülen. As Guida mentions, when this editor left, Bulaç went back to Zaman and "became closer to Fethullah Gülen's organization, as evidenced by his recent writings."[152] Bulaç worked for *Zaman* for a short period during the years 1993–1994; returning again in 1998 to remain until March 2016, when the newspaper was brought under state control with the accusation that the newspaper belonged to Fethullah Gülen's community, supported the formation of parallel structures, and undermined the government and the state.

Bulaç published texts in other pro-Islamist newspapers as well, such as *Milli Gazete* (National Newspaper),[153] *Yeni Devir* (New Era), and *Yeni Şafak* (New Dawn). In addition, he often appeared in debate and talk shows on TV channels of Islamic and Islamist orientation.[154] In 1998, he was honored with the "Thought Award" of the Turkish Authors' Association—an association which belongs to the circles of the Gülen community. Ali Bulaç has published dozens of books,[155] many of which have seen several editions.

---

149 Regarding the journal *Bilgi ve Hikmet*, see Ferhat Kentel, "1990'ların İslami Düşünce Dergileri": 729–34.

150 These are the following: Abdurrahman Arslan, Abdurrahman Dilpak, Ömer Çelik, Kadir Canatan, Ergün Yıldırım, Eyüp Koktaş, Mustafa Aydın, Ali Coşkun, Rasim Özdenören, Davut Dursun, Mehmet Bekaroğlu, and Ömer Dinçer.

151 For more, see Ferhat Kentel, "1990'ların İslami Düşünce Dergileri": 730.

152 Michelangelo Guida, "The New Islamists' Understanding": 352.

153 This is the newspaper that expresses and represents in a semi-formal way the Islamist movement of National View (Milli Görüş), which has been led by the Islamist politician Necmettin Erbakan until his death.

154 For instance, the channel *Mehtap TV*, which was founded in 2006; the channel *Hilal TV*, which was founded in 2005; the channel *TVNET*, which was founded in 2005 and belongs to the Albayrak Group of Companies, which also owns the newspaper *Yeni Şafak*.

155 Indicatively one should mention the following titles, the majority of which have been published several times: *Kuran-ı Kerim ve Türkçe Anlamı* (The Holy Quran and its

The most recent years in Bulaç's life and career have been marked by negative developments; in the first week of March 2016, the newspaper *Zaman,* as well as the (English-language) *Today's Zaman,* were set under state supervision and its directors and columnists were replaced—this being a measure taken by the Turkish government against the Gülen community. The newspaper was finally closed down in July 2016, a few days after the failed military coup (of July 15, 2016) in Turkey.

A warrant for his arrest was issued and Ali Bulaç turned himself in to police (on July 27, 2016); he and a number of other *Zaman* columnists were "accused of following exiled preacher Fethullah Gülen, whom the Turkish government accuses of maintaining a terrorist organization and "parallel state structure" (. . .) and masterminding a failed military coup on July 15, 2016."[156] Bulaç was released from pretrial detention on May 11, 2018; although the court imposed on him a travel ban and reporting requirements.[157] Finally on July 6, 2018, Bulaç was sentenced to eight years and eight months.[158]

Nevertheless, Bulaç's impact is considered to be important, not only on the educated young readership at which his texts are mainly directed, but also in political and party circles, as well as on other Islamist writers of his generation or younger. This has led Günter Seufert to write that Bulaç "represents the intellectual strand of Turkish Islamism of our times more than any other."[159] Bulaç has

---

Meaning in Turkish), *İslam Dünyasında Toplumsal Değişme* (Social Change in the Islamic World), *İslam Dünyasında Düşünce Sorunları* (Issues of Thought in the Islamic World), *Din ve Modernizm* (Religion and Modernism), *Modern Ulus Devlet* (The Modern Nation State), *Din Devlet ve Demokrasi* (Religion, State and Democracy), *Din ve Siyaset* (Religion and Politics).

156 See the report "Ali Bulaç" by the Committee to Protect Journalists (CPI); as it is mentioned there "According to records of the arraignment hearing (. . .) the state alleged that Bulaç, Alpay, Alkan, and Ünal wrote articles in Zaman praising FETÖ/PDY and the newspaper was the group's media organ." https://cpj.org/data/people/ali-bulac/ (accessed January 12, 2019).

157 See "Two FETÖ suspects released in Zaman daily case," *Hürriyet Daily News,* May 12, 2018, http://www.hurriyetdailynews.com/two-feto-suspects-released-in-zaman-daily-case-131706 (accessed January 12, 2019).

158 For instance, see the press release issued by Amnesty International UK on July 6, 2018, under the title "Turkey: 'Absurd' terror convictions of six journalists sends shock through media industry," https://www.amnesty.org.uk/press-releases/turkey-absurd-terror-convictions-six-journalists-sends-shock-through-media-industry (accessed January 12, 2019).

159 Günter Seufert, "Porträt Ali Bulaç".

had a great impact on the leading members of the Welfare Party (*Refah Partisi*) during the 1990s, a fact that induced painful consequences. As Yavuz writes:

> His writings have been quite influential. For example, Bahri Zengin, then deputy chairman of the RP, sought to place democracy within this Islamic framework by introducing into the election platform of the RP in 1995 Bulaç's concept of multilegal communities, which dates back to the Ottoman millet system, where each community was allowed to be ruled according to its own norms and laws. The Turkish Constitutional Court regarded the concept of "multilegal communities" as an indication of the RP's anti-secularism and banned the party.[160]

Bulaç's Islamist Thought

Bulaç's publishing house, *Düşünce*, published translated texts of important figures of the Islamist movement: the Iranians Ali Shariati and Ruhollah Khomeini, the Afghan Gulbuddin Hekmatyar, the Egyptian Muslim Brothers Hasan al-Banna and Sayyed Qutb, and the Pakistani Abul Ala Mawdudi.[161]

Bulaç's thought has been influenced to an extent by the writings and ideas of these important figures of the non-Turkish Islamist movement. His thought has also been influenced by the teachings of Said Nursi and Fethullah Gülen; he has published a book in favor of Fethullah Gülen,[162] while in an editorial text in *Zaman* (2005) he claimed—as Guida mentions—that "Gülen, like Mawdudi, Qutb, and Said Nursi, is an alim-enlightened because of his profound knowledge of Islamic and Western sciences."[163] As Anat Lapidot observes in her doctoral thesis, Bulaç is familiar with the work of Mawdudi and Shariati, but also with the work of Balzac and Dostojevski, as well as that of Marx, Hegel, and Weber.[164]

It is worth mentioning that in Bulaç's texts the influence of Mawdudi is apparently greater than that of Qutb and the Muslim Brothers; the reason for this should probably be attributed to the radical revolutionary stance of Qutb and the Muslim Brothers of Egypt. This assumption is reinforced by Guida, who

---

160 M. Hakan Yavuz, *Islamic Political Identity*, 119.

161 See Fatma Bostan Ünsal and Ertan Özensel, "Ali Bulaç", in *İslamcılık*, ed. Yasin Aktay, vol. 6 of *Modern Türkiye'de Siyasi Düşünce* (Istanbul: İletişim Yayınları, 2004), 739; Günter Seufert, "Porträt Ali Bulaç."

162 The book bears the title *Kutlu Ağaç* (published by Gazeteciler ve Yazarlar Vakfı Yayınları, İstanbul 2004) and contains Bulaç's articles published in the newspapers *Zaman* and *Yeni Şafak*. See Michelangelo Guida, "The New Islamists' Understanding": 352.

163 Michelangelo Guida, "The New Islamists' Understanding": 368, footnote 22.

164 See Anat Lapidot, *Islam and Nationalism*, 146 and 153.

writes: "As Bulaç recalled, the Arab world produced only militancy that does not really fit the post-1980 Turkish democratic context."[165]

The ideological impact of the Iranian Islamist intellectual Ali Shariati is also evident in Bulaç's thinking with respect to several matters: the necessity to disseminate and realize the true, authentic Islam; the duty of the intellectuals to enlighten youth and guide society;[166] the severe criticism of Western nations and states;[167] the importance of the unity of Islam and the classless character of society;[168] the emphasis placed on the doctrine of the unity of God (*tevhid*); and the need for Islam to be free from primitive non-Islamic practices and rituals that had penetrated it, which have created what Shariati negatively called "the Islam of the nobility, the official Islam, the ruling Islam, and Safavid Shi'ism."[169]

According to Lapidot, the ideological influence of Mawdudi and Shariati results from the fact that they "make greater use of modern concepts than their contemporaries, who tend to rely on the works of traditional medieval scholars as al-Ghazali."[170] In addition, Lapidot emphasizes the impact of Shariati's thought on Bulaç by underlining two main points: that Shariati perceived Islam as "a new sociological fact, a new practical Islam markedly different from the one about which the traditional preacher spoke," and that "Shariati and his Islamology[171] focus on harmony, social justice and personal liberation, all derived from the idea of *tevhid*, and all of which should be implemented in social and political life."[172] Furthermore, Lapidot finds common points between liberation theology

---

165 Michelangelo Guida, "The New Islamists' Understanding": 354. Guida notes also that "in the 1980s Bulaç matured as a writer" adding that "the turning point seems to be the September 12 military junta that closed down Düşünce. Bulaç himself was imprisoned for nearly 40 days." Ibid., 353.

166 See Ali Rahnema, *An Islamic Utopian: A Political Biography of Ali Shari'ati* (London: I.B. Tauris, 1998) 282 and 296.

167 "Shari'ati accuses the civilized nations of colonization, exploitation, enslavement, deception, injustice, corruption, aggression and war." Ali Rahnema, *An Islamic Utopian*, 203.

168 Ibid., 244.

169 Ibid., 283.

170 Anat Lapidot, *Islam and Nationalism*, 154.

171 As Rahnema notes, Islamology was a "progressive Islamic ideology." He adds the following: "Feeling the pressing need to enunciate a modernist and radical Islamic doctrine, which would compete with Marxism in attracting the young, whom he correctly believed were the engines of social change, Shari'ati halted all other academic projects and abruptly embarked on the articulation of his doctrine." Ali Rahnema, *An Islamic Utopian*, 282.

172 Anat Lapidot, *Islam and Nationalism*, 132.

and Bulaç's thought.[173] She observes that "there are four themes in the thought of the liberation theologians of Latin America (the critique of ideology, dependency theory, the preferential option for the poor, and the humans as the subject of history) all of which can be clearly identified in Ali Bulaç's work."[174] What seems to make Bulaç's work popular—as Lapidot writes—"is the dual commitment to view society from the perspective of the poor and powerless, and to give public witness of solidarity with their struggle for liberation."[175]

As it has been pointed out by Menderes Çınar and Ayşe Kadıoğlu, central to Bulaç's thinking and argumentation is the critique of modernity and its manifestations: secularism, individualism, the modern state, democracy, and freedom.[176] Çınar and Kadıoğlu maintain that Bulaç views and presents Islam as a "meta-narrative," as "the only religion that could constitute a frame of reference in building a pluralist society in the sense of a plurality of life styles."[177] In the words of Göle, "Bulaç seeks an 'alternative vision of the world' in Islam, arguing that 'politicization' and 'humanization' would lead to the impoverishment of Islam."[178]

A taste of Bulaç's vision is offered in his book *Çağdaş Kavramlar ve Düzenler* (Concepts and Orders of Our Times)[179] which was first published in the 1970s and is estimated to have sold over half a million copies by the mid 2000s.[180] This book became "the manifesto of the young Islamist movement in Turkey" according to Seufert, who observes: "The book drew a picture of Islam beyond

---

173 Christian theological and social movement, which originated in Latin America and aims at conquering social justice and liberating the poor from poverty, corruption and oppression, through the social and political mobilization of believers in the name of Christian faith: "[...] dating from the 1960s, liberation theology fuses concepts from the social sciences with biblical and theological ideas. In particular, in its use of Marxist and neo-Marxist social theory it may be superficially read both by undiscerning theologians and sympathetic sociologists as a form of radical social theory incorporating a secular ethic of justice. (...) There are a number of liberation theologies: black liberation theology, Jewish theology of liberation, Asian liberation theology, and Latin American liberation theology." *The Blackwell Dictionary of Modern Social Thought*, ed. William Outhwaite, 2nd ed. (Oxford: Blackwell Publishing, 2003), 349.
174 Anat Lapidot, *Islam and Nationalism*, 149.
175 Ibid., 150.
176 See Menderes Çınar and Ayşe Kadioğlu, "An Islamic Critique of Modernity": 62–63.
177 Ibid., 64.
178 Nilüfer Göle, *The Forbidden Modern*, 110.
179 Ali Bulaç, *Çağdaş Kavramlar ve Düzenler*, 20th ed. (Istanbul: İz Yayıncılık, 2007).
180 See Günter Seufert, "Porträt Ali Bulaç."

conservatism and nationalism, and depicted religion as an antidote to class conflicts and imperialism."[181] In this book, Bulaç argues against the government forms, political systems, ideologies, and concepts that the contemporary world has known: capitalism, Marxism and scientific socialism, fascism, conservatism, secularism and secularization, class society, and class divisions.[182] In other words, Bulaç seeks to point out and prove the superiority of Islam over all political ideologies and government systems that have been historically created in the Western world.[183]

At this point, a reference should be made to the influence exercised on Bulaç (as well as on many contemporary Islamist intellectuals in Turkey) by Kısakürek's thinking and the civilizational dimension he gave to Islam. One of the features of Kısakürek's Islamist thought was that he perceived Islam as a civilization; this perception serves as the basis for the comparison he made between Islam and the West, as two different worlds with different social, cultural, political, and religious foundations.[184]

It is a contrasting view of the Western and the Islamic civilization which has continued to be expressed in Turkey by conservative and Islamist writers; indeed, it could be said that it has been strengthened during the past two decades. In this theoretical framework, Islam and the West are two cultures that are characterized by different value systems and, therefore, they cannot be compatible.[185] Hence, the key to prosperity, progress, and justice in the Islamic world is not the imitation of the West or the adoption of Western values and institutions, but the

---

181 Ibid.
182 See the relevant chapters of the book in question.
183 As Meeker observes: "Notions like civilization, democracy, art, secularism, socialism, morality, spirituality, holiness, conservatism, rightism, feudalism, feminism, nationalism, communism, class, science, modernity, progress, nation, liberty, freedom, culture, tradition, backwardness, development and so on have all come from the West and are alien to an Islamic outlook. The Muslim intellectual will subject these concepts to systematic examination from an Islamic perspective." Michael Meeker, "The New Muslim Intellectuals", 200.
184 The so-called "civilization movement" within the Turkish intelligentsia was particularly noticeable during the 1950s and the 1960s. See Anat Lapidot, *Islam and Nationalism*, 151.
185 As a matter of fact, Ahmet Davutoğlu, who served as Prime Minister and Foreign Affairs Minister, dealt in his doctoral thesis with the Western and Islamic view of the world: Ahmet Davutoglu, *Alternative Paradigms: The Impact of Islamic and Western Weltanschauungs on Political Theory* (Lanham, Maryland: University Press of America, 1994).

revival and prosperity of Islam from within, from its very own values. This theoretical and intellectual background is dominant in the writings of Bulaç (and other writers of his generation).

The Role of the Muslim Intellectual

For Bulaç, as Meeker explains, "the Muslim intellectual is a new kind of believer who arises in response to the special challenges of contemporary life. His task is not to rework Islam so that it takes the form of yet one more modernist construction, but to show how its beliefs and practices remain a sufficient foundation for community in contemporary life."[186]

The Muslim intellectual (*aydın*) differs from the Muslim religious scholar (*alim*), as well as from the secular intellectual (*entelektüel*). The *alim* scholar is the one who "keeps secure the foundations of Muslim belief and practice through the study of Islamic sources," whereas "the secular intellectual is inspired by the Western image of a Prometheus who challenges divine authority, makes man the measure of everything and rises above the common people as a superman." The Muslim intellectual "is guided by a belief in the oneness of God and fear of God as he considers contemporary problems."[187]

As Meeker concisely writes with regard to Bulaç's perception of the role of Muslim intellectuals:

> [The book] *Intellectual Issues in the Islamic World* illustrates how in the present age the work of the Muslim intellectual complements the work of the Muslim scholar. While the Muslim intellectual looks primarily to contemporary life, the Muslim scholar looks primarily to the Koran, Hadith and Sharia. Working together, they will be able to harness contemporary life to right-thinking and right-acting. The special role and task of the Muslim intellectual, a thinker and writer who was not heretofore part of the Islamic community, is thereby conceived in terms of the project which inspired [the book] *Concepts and Orders of Our Time*. The Muslim intellectual is responding to the peculiar challenge of contemporary experience, a time when believers have been misled by all manner of modernist concepts and principles. The Muslim intellectual will serve to re-connect contemporary life with Islamic belief and practice, making possible a rebirth of the Islamic community.[188]

---

186 Michael Meeker, "The New Muslim Intellectuals", 201.
187 Ibid., 202.
188 Ibid., 202–3.

58   Ali Bulaç

In other words, as Çınar and Kadıoğlu put it, "Bulaç upholds the Muslim intellectuals as the heirs of the Prophet, in aiding the believers and non-believers in working their way out of modernity towards Islamic belief and practice."[189]

Typologies and Classifications of Islam

In his book *İslam ve Fundamentalizm* (Islam and Fundamentalism), Bulaç rejects as inadequate the suggestions or attempts by Western social scientists to offer a classification or typology of Islam.[190] He explains the reason for this as follows:

> (...) they made their appearance within the characteristic conditions of another cultural climate. If they are used with limited goals, they can be explanatory and useful. Yet, we have to consider if they can have such a broad application that they can create categories within a religion which is The Religion, and describe the occult fields that have formed the foundations of a belief, the epistemology of a kind of holistic life and a perception of the Universe, like Islam.[191]

Bulaç advocates a different view of the history of Islam, which should be based on the notions of *kitap* (book) and *ümmet* (Islamic community of believers). By using the terms *Kitabi İslam* (Islam of the Book) and *Ümmi İslam* (Islam of the community of believers), he intends to show that Islam has followed, historically, two paths: one which follows the written sources, and one which evolves and is experienced within the society of believers. In other words, the former is the Islam of lawmakers and political power, while the latter is the Islam of oral tradition and society.[192] By elaborating his argumentation further, he reaches the conclusion that the sole path to the prosperity of Muslims is the conjuncture of these two trends of Islam. The representatives of *Kitabi İslam*, that is, the *ulema* and the intellectuals, with their knowledge and their writings, can offer concrete, modern, and practical solutions to problems and concerns of *Ümmi*

---

189 Menderes Çinar and Ayşe Kadioğlu, "An Islamic Critique of Modernity": 64.
190 See Ali Bulaç, *İslam ve Fundamentalizm* (Istanbul: İz Yayıncılık, 1997), 104–21. More concretely, he rejects "the various approaches and representations of Islam that have prevailed in social science as pairs of opposing and different perceptions and expressions – with the aim of understanding the societies and the history of Islam– as follows: a) the example of 'center - periphery', b) the example of 'populist Islam - elitist Islam', c) the example of 'political Islam - cultural Islam', d) the example of 'high Islam - low Islam'." Konstantinos Gogos, *Turkish Political Islam*, 102.
191 Ali Bulaç, *İslam ve Fundamentalizm*, 121.
192 Ibid., 121–26.

İslam, in other words, of the Muslim community, and accordingly they can guide Muslims.[193]

The above-mentioned references contribute to a better understanding of Bulaç's wider intellectual and explanatory context about Islam and Islamic society and, additionally, they confirm the leading role that he assigns to the intellectuals (and himself) of the Muslim world.

The Islamist Movement

Bulaç's perception of the Islamist movement is of particular importance, not only because he has for decades been a leading public intellectual in Turkey but also because this perception demonstrates a way of thinking that originates from within the Muslim world, and Turkey in particular. When referring to the Islamist movement, the Turkish Islamist intellectual uses the notion of 'Islamism' (*İslamcılık*), in a relevant text of his.[194] He differentiates the meaning and the content of Islamism from that of Islam with the following words:

> What we mean here is not Musulmanism as a religion, but the entire ideological and political production which was created through a movement – from the general parameters of this religion – by a part of Muslims (educated circles, political classes and social leaders) who express in this religion their concerns and their bonds. We can regard this as a kind of 'reading' of Islam under the material and social conditions of the contemporary world. We can call those ones, in short, 'Islamists' (*İslamcılar*).[195]

Bulaç seeks to explain what he means by writing the following:

> Islamism can be defined, on the one hand, as the work of the social group of cultural, political and social leaders – who appear in various fields of activity with concrete demands and clear claims – with the aim to ensure the creation of a world that matches the spiritual, ethical, cultural, and social values of Musulmanism, and on the other hand, as the attempts on various levels and in various fields to achieve this goal. The most important thing that differentiates the "Islamists" from the others and from other - typical for contemporary times - historical categories, is that their point of reference is Musulmanism as a religion and that they clearly prioritize the Muslim identity. There is no doubt that in a Muslim country or society, people are Muslims, but the "Islamists" have restated the beliefs and the cultural values of the people, which cannot be expressed

---

193 Ibid., 126. See also Konstantinos Gogos, *Turkish Political Islam*, 103.
194 Ali Bulaç, "İslam'ın Üç Siyaset Tarzı veya İslamcıların Üç Nesli", in *İslamcılık*, ed. Yasin Aktay, vol. 6 of Modern Türkiye'de Siyasi Düşünce (Istanbul: İletişim Yayınları, 2004), 48–67.
195 Ali Bulaç, "İslam'ın Üç Siyaset Tarzı", 50.

in a specific conceptual framework, sometimes by restoring them to their origins, sometimes by rejecting them or by submitting them to a selection procedure.[196]

In addition, Bulaç underlines that the social and political profile of an Islamist is
different than that of an *ulema*;[197] he holds that the Islamist movement, from its
beginning until today, is marked by three historical periods:

> Islamism is not a political and ideological current that appeared at a historical moment
> and moved within history. It is a procedure that was cultivated, evolved and reproduced
> itself in every new situation. In order to understand Islamism, we have to deal with this
> issue on the basis of generations [throughout time] and not resort to any horizontal
> division. Thus, I believe that it will be more enlightening for the understanding of the
> adventure and history of Islamism to take as basis the religious, cultural and political
> views of the three different Islamist generations.[198]

The Islamist generations (or phases) in question, as perceived by Bulaç, are
the first (1856–1924), the second (1950–2000), and the third Islamist generation (after 2000).[199] With regard to the first period of the Islamist movement, he
explains that Islamism emerged as a reaction to the new structures brought by
the Ottoman Reform Edict of 1856 (*Islahat Fermanı*), while the year 1924 marks
the political and institutional elimination both of the Islamists and the Ottoman
state. The Islamists of this period called for renewal (*tecdit*), reform (*ıslah*), or
revival (*ihya*).

During the second period of Islamism (1950–2000) both Turkey and the
Muslim world experienced huge migration waves from the countryside to the
urban areas, which altered social structures. This period is marked—as Bulaç
writes—by the Islamists' aim:

> to Islamize not only state and institutions but society and cultural structures. The year
> 1950 is indicative for the political and social changes that took place in Turkey and the
> Muslim world: in 1946 Turkey entered a new era of multi-party politics; in 1947 Pakistan
> was established as a Muslim nation state; in those years the Muslim Brotherhood shaped
> its political identity in Egypt, while in 1953 the Mossadegh movement signaled a radical
> change in the political thought of Muslims.[200]

---

196 Ibid.
197 Ali Bulaç, "İslam'ın Üç Siyaset Tarzı", 50–51.
198 Ibid., 51.
199 Ali Bulaç, "İslam'ın Üç Siyaset Tarzı", 48–50. For a discussion of his main points see
     Konstantinos Gogos, "Turkish Islamist Intellectuals", 431–35.
200 Ali Bulaç, "İslam'ın Üç Siyaset Tarzı", 49.

Regarding the third phase of the Islamist movement, Bulaç explains that the year 2000 is not the exact year that signals the beginning of a new stage of the Islamist movement in various Muslim states, but is used indicatively to illustrate the changes that took place just before or after the year 2000. As far as Turkey is concerned, the beginning of the third Islamist phase is placed by Bulaç already in the 1990s, since in that decade the Islamist movement was strengthened and consolidated in the form of a political party. In this respect, he notes the following:

> By the end of the 1990s, apparently, the demands of society and the people brought on significant Islamic political formations. In Turkey, in 1995 the Welfare Party came first in the elections, but after governing for one year it was forced to resign from power (post-coup [sic] of February 28th). At the same time, in Iran the Islamists of the second generation experienced a big electoral defeat by the Islamists of the third generation, i.e. the Khatami group.[201]

In his opinion, the main characteristics and causes that led to a distinctive third phase of the Islamist movement in the Muslim world have been the completion of the urbanization and the globalization processes, and additionally—regarding Turkey in particular—the European Union membership process.[202]

The Medina Document

Yet, what is it exactly that Bulaç proposes to his readers? He advocates for the establishment of an Islamic society—and an Islamic order—that will bear the characteristics of the first Muslim society which, according to Bulaç, had been realized at the very beginning of Islamic history, that is, the era of Islam's just order.[203]

Bulaç holds that the just order of the first Islamic era was achieved and guaranteed by the Medina Document (known also as Medina Contract, or the Constitution of Medina), "a contract signed by the Prophet Muhammad, Jews, and polytheists granting Muslims the right to rule in the Arabian city and at the same time protecting the rights of other groups."[204] At that time, "10,000 people lived in Medina, of which 1,500 were Muslims, 4,000 were Jews and 4,500 were

---

201 Ibid., 50.
202 Ibid., 49–50.
203 See Michael Meeker, "The New Muslim Intellectuals", 197–205; Nermin Abadan-Unat, "Ideologische Strömungen": 296–97; Konstantinos Gogos, "Turkish Islamist Intellectuals", 425.
204 Ali Bulaç, "The Medina Document", in *Liberal Islam: A Sourcebook*, ed. Charles Kurzman (New York: Oxford University Press, 1998), 169.

Polytheist Arabs."[205] According to Bulaç, the Medina Document must be seen as a document of great practical political and legal importance. He argues the following:

> The document concerned is not an artificial utopia or a theoretical political exercise. It has entered written history as a legal document employed systematically and concretely from 622 to 632.
>
> The principles of this legal document establish the framework of political unity, and the meanings they bestow upon the concepts of politics and power are still important today. Briefly defined, the Medina Document is the legal manuscript for political unity. The general framework of this document presents itself as a social project [for Islamic intellectuals today].[206]

As has been noted (already in the 1960s), the document "appears to be authentic but there is uncertainty about its date."[207] It could have taken its final form after the summer of 627, though it contains older articles.[208] Nevertheless, in an attempt to underline the diachronic value of this agreement for Muslims, Bulaç stresses the following:

> For a Muslim, the desire to live according to the divine legal order of Islam never diminishes. On the contrary, as he enters more and more into the universe of knowledge of the religion to which he belongs, this desire increases. Besides this, the second big task of a Muslim is to promulgate to others the truths of the religion, which he accepts as the source of all Truth. A Muslim can never avoid or neglect this duty... If a Muslim can fulfill this dual mission within the social organization he finds himself in, he is powerful. The final objective of the difficult struggle that filled the lives of all prophets and the final Prophet Muhammad, peace be upon him, was to make possible the free milieu, the conducive social environment where this mission can realize itself. What Muslims understand of *freedom*[209] is nothing but the eradication of the obstacles that prevent them from living their religion completely and promulgating it to others...[210]

According to Bulaç, apart from the ideal Islamic society that was realized during the years of the Prophet through the Medina Document, the Ottomans had applied a similar social and legal organization in the form of the *millet* system. He holds that even nowadays, the ideal type of social organization and order can

---

205 Ibid., 170.
206 Ibid., 176.
207 W. Montgomery Watt, *Muhammad: Prophet and Statesman* (Oxford: Oxford University Press, 1964), 93.
208 Ibid., 94.
209 In the original text the word "freedom" is in italics.
210 Ali Bulaç, "The Medina Document", 177.

be achieved only through a co-federation of religious-cultural communities and not through an organization based on nations, states, and individuals/citizens.[211] Bulaç believes that the solution for the co-existence of various communities in modern Turkey lies in a multi-judicial system of communities. He advocates the establishment of a social and legal organization (similar to the Medina Document) in Turkey—and in other Muslim states as well—which, always according to Bulaç, will allow the various communities have their own structures with regard to religion, language, culture, art, and education and will result in less tension and conflict. In conclusion, as Bulaç writes, "the Medina Document is the source of a blueprint that may be an alternative to a modern state that is becoming more totalitarian, overtly and covertly, through raw or sophisticated methods and means."[212]

However, Bulaç's view about the application of the basic principles of the Medina Document in the present-day world cannot be received without reasonable criticism, mainly because of the different circumstances that prevail nowadays in all fields of social and political life and state organization. Guida has emphasized the need to analyze and understand the Medina Document historically, within its historical time and circumstances.[213]

Further, it can be said that Bulaç's societal project has indeed considerable deficiencies and problems. Çınar and Kadıoğlu have already pointed out a number of them: Bulaç "looks backward and introduces a societal model which cannot cope with the complexities of modern societies"; in his envisioned societal project "the individual is rather passive, since s/he does not develop her/his capacities by participation"; and although he rejects human reason as a basic element of modernity, his model is based on human reason; he sees Islam as

---

211 For an extensive treatment of the features of the state organization according to the Medina Document, see Ali Bulaç, *Modern Ulus Devlet*, 2nd ed. (Istanbul: İz Yayıncılık, 1998), 195–232. About the ideas of Ali Bulaç, see Fatma Bostan Ünsal and Ertan Özensel, "Ali Bulaç", 736–57.

212 Ali Bulaç, "The Medina Document", 178.

213 "Critics of Bulaç, believed that the "Constitution of Medina" was indeed an original and authoritative source, yet it had to be analyzed historically, in the light of political events of the late Medina period. When the agreement was signed, Muslims were fleeing from Mecca, a city whose inhabitants were hostile to the tiny Muslim minority. A few years later the situation changed dramatically, and the Constitution became a "historical text": after a few years, all the minorities disappeared from the city, and relations with minorities in other parts of the Arab Peninsula were always unbalanced; Sharīʿa indeed dominated all aspects of life." Michelangelo Guida, "The New Islamists' Understanding": 356.

the "only universal religion which tolerates differences; such a view of toleration produces a humiliation of the tolerated."[214]

Bulaç's Writings

Text: "A Method of Conciliation in Tunisia"[215]

Bulaç wrote extensively during the 1990s about the Medina Document and brought it to the foreground of Islamist argumentation in Turkey. Ever since, he has never stopped referring to it and its advantages for current conditions. A characteristic example of how Bulaç perceives such a social and political settlement nowadays can be seen in the following text, published in *Today's Zaman*, in December 2015:

> The Nobel Peace Prize for 2015 was awarded to the Tunisian National Dialogue Quartet: the Tunisian General Labor Union (UGTT), the Tunisian Confederation of Industry, Trade and Handicrafts (UTICA), the Tunisian Human Rights League (LTDH), and the Tunisian Order of Lawyers. I was curious about what they did to deserve the prize. These four organizations saved Tunisia from a serious crisis. The method they adopted to pave the way for conciliation is of great interest to me.
>
> As Tunisian Order of Lawyers President Muhammad Fadil Mahfud explained, it wasn't a walk in the park to bring together political parties with diverse political programs and huge differences. The Ennahda Movement had been in power for about two years and the Nidaa Tounes party and other parties had virtually united against it. The Ennahda government was legitimate, as it had come to power democratically. However, having overthrown a strong autocratic administration, many groups not only sought to get their voices heard, but also ensure their demands and programs are represented in the administration.
>
> Political parties and civil society organizations are sociological structures. It is impossible to suppress political or civil movements, sects, religious communities or groups using legal measures; being under duress does not mean that they are destroyed or that they have abandoned their views or demands.
>
> What had drawn me to the idea that a political union could be formed and the public sphere arranged through conciliation or contracts within the framework of the Charter of Medina - an agreement drafted by the Prophet Muhammad as a formal agreement between him and all of the significant tribes and families of Yathrib (later known as Medina), including Muslims, Jews and pagans - is the sociological nature of political and civil movements. Given the impossibility of destroying or suppressing sociological elements, the best way is to establish a "contractual society" in which everyone can

---

214 Menderes Çinar and Ayşe Kadioğlu, "An Islamic Critique of Modernity": 68–69.
215 Published in the online edition of *Today's Zaman*, December 6, 2015.

maintain their creedal, social and political existence without attempting to attain absolute domination over others.

The Tunisian National Dialogue Quartet started by forming a national conciliation and dialogue commission based on four principles: (a) determination to reach an agreement, (b) readiness to make compromises, (c) mutual negotiation and (d) patience. Their departure point was this: As no political force can shape the country or society alone, we are obliged to come to terms and make a compromise in order to avert domestic conflict or a new repressive regime. For conciliation or consensus, the parties involved have to make concessions. Mutual negotiation, discussion and bargaining should be employed in building a country or society. In this process, the parties involved should not only tolerate each other, but also be patient until they attain their ultimate goal peacefully.

Civil society organizations and political parties were the two pillars of the conciliation that would be attained through dialogue and consensus. This was achieved to a certain extent, and Tunisia was saved from a bloody coup d'état as occurred in Egypt, as well as from a civil war as is the case in Syria.

I was excited to hear about this method. The method I developed through my studies on the holy Quran, the Prophet's traditions (hadith), and the Charter of Medina for establishing the political unity and regulating the public life is based on three principles: making acquaintance, negotiating and making a covenant. In the first place, the parties involved should get acquainted with each other. In the second phase, they express their views, demands and visions, and negotiate with each other over them. In the final stage, they make a civil, social or political/legal contract. The world will eventually get tired of conflicts and head toward this method. It may eventually break up, but it is quite significant that this model worked in Tunisia, albeit on a small scale.

Text: "Europe Should Not Isolate Itself"[216]

There are some important reasons behind tension Europe is experiencing with foreigners. Some relate to historical and religious factors while others are connected to the level of socioeconomic welfare. Political and military factors that cause conflict and tension, too, can be added to this list. Yet there is a plain truth: In the past, European countries failed to develop multi-religious, multi-ethnic political structures – contrary to what Muslim states did. When Protestantism emerged as an interpretation of Christianity different from Catholicism, wars and massacres followed. One-third of the continent's population lost its life in this process. During that time, there existed not only different sects of Islam, but also different religions under the rule of Muslim states. In a sense, what gave Islam its dynamism in history was its ability to develop multi-religious, multi-ethnic social models.

---

216 Part of the text that was published in the online edition of *Today's Zaman*, September 18, 2009.

Today, there are two major problems facing the West: First, the West is extremely self-confident of its culture – therefore enjoying the false belief that there is nothing it can learn from other societies; and second, the West does not care for the problems, famine, or poverty [in] other parts of the world as it tries to preserve its standard of life. Europe and more generally the West have responsibilities toward non-Western world. They have to fulfill these responsibilities by opening to the external world and treating it as their equals.

Text: "What We Get from the West, and How to Use it"[217]

The Islamic world is obliged to undergo a deep-rooted and all-embracing change. It cannot continue in its current form. No one is denying this. However, there is a reality which both the West and our intellectuals must accept: The Islamic world can change only in accordance with its own inner dynamics and points of reference. Attempts at reform which have come in from the outside world and been imposed form the West over the past 200 years have remained as state and government projects, due to the unwillingness of the powerful elite to engage in democratic processes, which is, in turn, why these attempts at reform are not usually internalized by society as a whole. Those who set out with the goal of changing this situation first need to think carefully before taking steps. Unfortunately, what happens in Turkey is what we first take steps forward, and then start thinking. This could be seen as a bit of an Ottoman tradition.

Of course, in making reforms, we will reap benefits from the West. But we also need to make some interventions into our conceptual framework. The key concepts arising from Western or other cultural wealth of experiences naturally include world views, philosophies and background plans which are directly related to other nations' institutions and political structures. If we simply import these concepts without altering them, they cannot help us; these are concepts which need to be arranged according to our own physical, social and historical development. After all, the Quran itself changed some of the meanings in the language of the society to which it came. While Arabic words maintained the same form, their meaning underwent deep-rooted changes. Likewise, the philosopher Farabi borrowed some basic concepts from Greek metaphysics and philosophy, altering them, and even re-defining some entirely. Had Muslim scholars not done this, Greek philosophy would have remained an archaic resource, and would have been useless in the creation of modern language.

It was in the 19th century that this opportunity presented itself to us. But the figures of the Tanzimat, the Meşrutiyet and the Republic eras of Turkey all formed their relations with the West on a symbolic level, not thinking to form relations on a conceptual level. It was Sultan Mahmut II who first formed these incorrect relations: borrowing jazz music, offering alcoholic drinks at official meetings, changing outfits, replacing the sarık with the fez, then later the fez with the hat, banning the headscarf, intervening in the wearing

---

217 Published in the online edition of *Today's Zaman*, October 9, 2009.

of beards by men, and so on. These were all models accepted in the 20th century which derived from Mahmut II.

I talked a bit above about the relations between the Abbasis and Greek philosophy, and how it was not on the level of "awe and symbols" but rather on a smart and conceptual level. This was true also for their relations with Indian, Babylonian, Egyptian and Mesopotamian cultures. Note that Muslims did not translate Greek literature, mythology, tragedies and poetry into Arabic. They translated instead the philosophy and knowledge. Their goal in doing this was to benefit from the wealth of experience and knowledge of other cultures and civilizations, and to use their own religion and abilities to engage in their own semantic changes to all this. Looked at from this perspective, the modernization of Ottoman-Turk was unsuccessful; it cannot be an example to this Islamic world. What we need to take instead as an example is the above-mentioned Abbasi model.

We could use these Abbasi methods today to help us in finding solutions and providing new frameworks through which to interpret and understand our problems with democracy, civil society, and so on. Of course, this does not mean we will simply affect whichever changes grab us at the moment with these concepts. But at the same time, we ought not to simply import concepts from the West as they are and should instead alter and shape them according to our own culture, history and society. When we grapple with the process of societal change, and deal, with it according to this sort of framework, then we can use our own inner dynamics to change.

Text: "Role of Religion in Politics"[218]

We are surely going through a deep crisis; this should not be overlooked or ignored. It is because just as there are no historical classes in the Turkish and Islamic world, there are also no historical ideologies.

The rehabilitation of the masses that migrated from rural areas to urban sites following the Industrial Revolution, starting in 1750, was not so easy. Severe crises were experienced in the Western world but owing to large amounts of wealth transferred from the colonies to their respective empires, the labor class was successfully integrated into the system. Currently, we have to consider the painful experiences and historical process that the Western world went through when we insist that the entire world should become like the Western countries. One-third of the entire European population disappeared in sectarian violence in continental Europe alone. The West's only achievement, owing to some favorable historical conditions, is its having had the ability to find a point of reconciliation. Constitutional movements and multiparty political regimes refer to the reconciliation achieved at the end of class wars.

---

218 Published in the online edition of *Today's Zaman*, June 13, 2008. This text was not included in the Greek version of the book; it has been added here in order to better demonstrate Bulaç's thinking and argumentation.

The failure to properly read and interpret our history and social development dynamics lies behind many of our current problems. Our notions and models that enable us to think were transferred from other societies, just like our laws and attire. This seriously undermines our self-perspective toward ourselves. Of course, we must benefit extensively from the West's experience. Of course, we must import a lot of things from European countries and adapt them to our conditions. But this is not what we do; we only translate and transfer the imported assets. This is the primary reason for the current deadlock in relation to the regulation of political models and social life based on a just and fair political approach. As pointed out by Sait Halim Pasha, an important political thinker and intellectual of the late Ottoman era, our social structure has been shaped based on religion (socio-cultural criteria) -- and not on class principles (socioeconomic criteria). This implies that religious, ethnic and cultural identity have been considered very important criteria and values in our history. In short, because there is no understanding of class in our tradition, we have never experienced the influence of a historical class ideology (bourgeoisie or proletariat). The political parties that bear labels such as liberal, conservative, socialist, social democrat and nationalist fail to represent the masses, the cultural and economic victims of the political system, simply because they are formed by urban elites rather than the peripheral actors. In this case, migrants from rural areas to urban cities realize that their identities and lifestyles are under threat and that their living conditions are exacerbated due to increased inequality and the huge gap between the bureaucratic center and the big capital circles.

In such a combination, Islam appears as a method of politics and a comprehensive means of opposition because there is no alternative to embrace the masses seeking democratic participation. The class politics designed to bring a certain class into office operates to maximize the interests of that class. Because there has been no historical class in the Islamic world, value-oriented politics stands out -- and there is nothing more natural than this.

The reliance of some contemporary Islamic movements on violence is only sporadic and may not be taken as a general tendency. Their actions, resembling those of the Kharijites, stem from the temporary inability to adapt to the environment following the recent move to urban areas. The scholars and intellectuals with Western-style educational backgrounds who fail to read the cultural codes of their societies properly describe the new inhabitants of the urban cities as migrant and wild, whereas they also criticize them, asking why they fail to adapt to the nationalization project wherein their identities are denied and they are given an inferior position. But isn't this what is contrary to human nature?

Text: "The Codes of Politics"[219]

Parties in Turkey, whether they are right or left wing, differ from the parties in the West which have emerged out of the criteria of social class. They conduct politics taking into

---

219 Part of the text that was published in the online edition of *Today's Zaman*, July 21, 2009.

consideration identities which have arisen from the class structure. This is a certain pathology inherent to this.

The second important issue is that when parties conduct politics with an identity based on class criteria in a society that does not have classes, they end up belonging to the center or the state. These parties may appear to be conducting politics for the people; however, these parties, in reality, can't help but conduct politics on behalf of the state.

In Turkey, the center and the core of the center is made up of the following factors: the military, civilian bureaucracy, justice, major capital, university and intellectuals. These five elements, which combined create the core of Turkey's center, are most like an atomic nucleus. The center, however, is made up of centrifugal forces and showcases the desire to conduct politics based on religion.

Although unspoken, in Turkey and the Islamic world, only Islamist movements and parties conduct politics based on values. The others, let us take the nationalists as an example, conduct politics based on race, ethnicity, at times class, clan and family. There is a paradoxical situation taking place here; politics based on values encompass all classes and sees that all owners of rights, including the rich, are given their rights. It is based on justice and principle. For example, according to Marxist theory, the bourgeoisie never improve, they commit suicide. There is a suicide of class in Marxism, according to the Islamic perspective, everyone can attain value. And the highest value in politics is justice.

Text: "Islamist Kemalists"[220]

Unlike a commonly held approach and view, Islam is not just a religion; and as opposed to other religions, it is actually "the" religion.

In other words, it is a religion that sustains and preserves the sacred teachings, ancient teachings, essence and virtuous legacies of former religions. In the end, we can find the transcendental unity and message of the former religions in Islam and its teachings because Islam basically underlines that all prophets rely on the same divine message and that Prophet Muhammad is the last messenger and prophet of God; Islam also tells its followers not to make any distinction between the prophets and apostles of God (Quran, 2:285).

But the Muslim mindset is so confused that there are Muslim materialists who argue that there are no transcendental dimensions in Islam. They uphold that the reason Muslims are backward is because the Muslims who initially paid attention to the material world and material progress were taken hostage by the myths and legends of the Iranian, Indian, Greek and Christian civilizations. They further argue that Sufism and mysticism are one of the most important factors of this backwardness. Some Arab nationalists present Islam as an Arab religion, arguing that the Prophet Muhammad was an Arab and that the Quran was revealed in the Arabic language; some Turkish nationalists, on the

---

220 Published in the online edition of *Today's Zaman*, September 20, 2015.

other hand, respond to this argument noting that the Turks served Islam better. If you ask the Persians, they would probably argue that progress in Islam was made possible by the involvement of the Persians in the process. Most probably, in the near future, Kurdish nationalists will also refer to Muslim-Kurdish scholars and Salahuddin Ayyubi as greater contributors to Islam.

What is striking in these approaches is that Islam is detached from its genuine context and exploited for other goals and policies. After the adoption of the nation-state model by Muslims without reservations, all attempted to exploit Islam for their own goals. Some adopted Islam as a founding element and legitimized their presence with reference to it; some used it as a secondary element to convince the people that their attempts were justifiable. For instance, Wahhabi Islam is the main factor that legitimizes the Saudi regime. In Turkish nationalism, Islam is regarded as one of the elements that create a nation. It should be noted that the role of Islam in the determination of the national identity also determines its value. Undoubtedly, Mustafa Kemal was prone to a type of Islamism defended by Jamaluddin al-Afghani at the beginning. But then he agreed on a secular model because of the influence of external and internal factors. But if he had believed that Islam would have served the goals of the Turkish nation-state, he would have used Islam as a tool. Mustafa Kemal's practices and thoughts suggest that he sought to use the opportunities of an Islamist modernization model by relying on a Protestant religion. It is an irony to see that the current Islamist Kemalists also pay attention to Islam in an attempt to implement a similar project.

Conclusion

As Bulaç is regarded as a popular and leading Turkish Islamist intellectual, his texts can shed light on his way of thinking and ideas, as well as on the way of thinking and views of his educated readership in Turkey. As a matter of fact, his main target is exactly this readership. The quoted passages in this chapter aimed at showing some basic characteristics of his thought on issues regarding the political and social organization, Islam and the Islamist movement, the relations between Islam and the West, and state and democracy in Turkey and the Middle East.

It is obvious from his writings that Bulaç is caustic and fiercely critical of the civilization, ideas, and history of the West. Nevertheless, it should be underlined that his approach is often highly influenced by Western social and historical notions and references. Further to this, it appears that Bulaç himself cannot always fully apply the intellectual frameworks or proposals he presents as an antidote to the West and the Western exemplar. For instance, the following paradox is easily noticed: while he rejects the categorizations and the labels that are attributed to or refer to Islam and Islamism as inappropriate and wrong, he uses the terms "Islamism" and "Islamist movement" in exactly the same way as many Western scholars and researchers do—as well as many scholars in the Muslim world.

It might still be possible to say that Bulaç expresses and represents the cultural trend of the Islamist movement; that he is a "cultural Islamist" in other words. Though it should be clear that he is an Islamist writer, and that his Islamist way of thinking has not only a cultural orientation, but also evident and strong political and socio-political orientations. Even if one may use the adjective "cultural" before Bulaç's Islamism, this does not mean that Bulaç's (political-ideological) criticism of the West and Western institutions, of Western states and their policies, of modernity and its aspects, and of the perceived enemies of Islam or of non-Islamic attitudes and actions is lukewarm.

Bulaç's belief that Islam is superior to all the political systems and ideologies that the Western world has produced and experienced (as well as to the knowledge produced in and by the West) is a common theme in the thought and worldview of Islamists, either intellectuals or politicians, revealing a strong Occidentalism (to be understood as reversed Orientalism).

Nevertheless, I would like to underline the following: in many cases, Bulaç invokes historical facts and historical consequences in order to justify his criticism of the Western world and civilization, and to prove the superiority of the Muslim world and Islam. However, in this case it is evident that very often he adopts an achronic approach to history, according to which he is able, for example, to refer to the Crusades in order to prove the permanent and radical hostility between Muslims and Western Christianity (both in the past and today), to prove the barbarity of the Christian West against the developed and civilized Muslim East, and to justify contemporary anti-Western stances. In this specific example though, another very obvious problem is that such an approach and argumentation does not take Byzantium into account, which was Christian and which also suffered severely from the (Christian) crusaders—this would show that the Christian world was not, entirely and absolutely, an uncivilized crusader, destroyer, and conqueror of the Muslim world (as Islamist writers want to prove) and that the Muslim world was not the sole victim of the Crusades or other disasters.

When dealing with questions related to the history and the relations between the Muslim and the Western world, even when dealing with questions of Turkish interest or issues related to the Middle East, Bulaç's thought is bipolar. This is typical of the Islamist ideological framework and perception, in the sense that its core is dominated by the rivalry between Islam and the West. Besides this, he makes a crucial mistake: he views Europe and the West (with its history, science, civilization, religion, and ideologies) as a compact and monolithic sphere, without differentiations or dividing lines; for example, without differentiating between Western Medieval Christian societies and Byzantine society, or between Western European states and Czarist Russia in modern times; without the differentiation between conquerors and conquered in various periods of European history, or between developed and non-developed societies and states.

Bulaç strongly supports the re-organization of contemporary Muslim societies according to the Constitution of Medina, i.e. a model of societal organization that allows for the parallel existence of different communities and minorities, each of which is organized according to its own legal system and its own cultural or national specific features. He advocates an upgraded sociopolitical role for (cultural and religious) communities in current times. As a matter of fact, this is not at all irrelevant to Bulaç's relationship with the Gülen movement, which is in short referred to as "community" (*cemaat*) in Turkey.

His proposal entails at least two major disadvantages: the first one is that, taking into account their geographical boundaries, their institutions, as well as their economic and social structures, contemporary states constitute entities that are much more complex than the city of Medina during the first years of Islam.[221] To what extent could the organizational model of Medina be applied in a contemporary state? This would mean a restriction of the role of the state in fundamental policy areas, and the reinforcement of autonomy and self-organization of religious or cultural communities or social groups within a state. To what extent would that be feasible and what would the possible consequences be?

The second major disadvantage has to do with the observation that religious identity and religious belonging is crucial for the multi-legal social structure that Bulaç suggests. However, nowadays there are many individuals who do not identify themselves according to religion or religious identity, who do not wish to belong to any religious community. Nonetheless, "Bulaç failed to understand that the structure of *cemaats* puts certain cultural and social restrictions on the individual that limit personal freedoms".[222] What is meant is that, in such a case, the individual will enjoy fewer freedoms and will be subject to more restrictions than within a democratically organized political and social structure. In other words, it is not obvious in what way and to what extent the organizational structure of multi-legal communities can be better than the existing model of Western democracy and the democratic state.

---

221 For this observation, see Michelangelo Guida, "The New Islamists' Understanding": 367.
222 Ibid., 355.

Even with regard to the Ottoman Empire, which Bulaç views as a successful application of the system of multi-legal communities, he fails to convince us that the millet system was a perfect organizational structure for all subjects (especially for non-Muslims) of the empire. Besides this, it can also be noted that if Bulaç himself regards the example of the Tunisian Quartet as a contemporary practical application of the Medina Document, this application is far from Bulaç's theoretical premise and perception.

Be that as it may, the idea and the project of multi-legal communities can be attractive for many Islamists and can be expected to constitute in future a topic of discussion or suggestions by Islamist intellectuals or politicians, both in the Middle East and Europe.

Chapter 4 Abdurrahman Dilipak

Short Biography

Abdurrahman Dilipak was born in 1949 in Haruniye/Düziçi,[223] a city situated close to Adana. In Adana, he attended an *İmam Hatip* school. In terms of higher education, he started studying Arabic and Persian Literature at the University of Istanbul. However, he never graduated from that department, changing his field of study and graduating from the Department of Journalism and Public Relations of the Academy of Economic and Commercial Sciences (*İktisadi ve Ticari İlimler Akademisi*) instead. He is married and the father of four children, two boys and two girls.[224]

As far as his work and professional trajectory is concerned, Dilipak himself stated (in 2009) the following: "For forty years now, I have been a writer. I have done television programs. I give lectures. I am a Human Rights and Peace activist. I paint. For some time, I was involved in the movies. I have been put on hundreds of trials."[225]

Dilipak's Publishing Activity and Writings

Throughout his career as a journalist, Dilipak served as editor of various newspapers and publications of the Islamic movement. He was one of the founders of the (Islamist) newspaper *Yeni Devir* (New Era), while he maintained his own column about foreign policy issues in the newspaper *Milli Gazete* (National Newspaper). Furthermore, he has written for other publications, such as the weekly newspaper *Vahdet* (Unity) and the journal *Cuma* (Friday).[226] It should be noted that, in ideological and political terms, the newspaper *Milli Gazete*[227] is closely linked to the Islamist movement of Milli Görüş (National

---

223 The current name of the city is Düziçi, however Dilipak shows preference to its Ottoman-Arabic name: Haruniye. See interview "Veysel Tepeli'nin Abdurrahman Dilipak ile yaptığı röportaj," *Adana Medya*, May 29, 2009, http://www.adanamedya. com/veysel-tepelinin-abdurrahman-dilipak-ile-yaptigi-roportaj-15345h.htm (accessed February 10, 2016).
224 Ibid.
225 Ibid.
226 See the short biographical résumé cited in his book *Laisizm* (2nd ed. Istanbul: Beyan Yayınları, 1991)
227 For more information, see Konstantinos Gogos, *Turkish Political Islam*, 353–59.

View), which was founded by Necmettin Erbakan and formed the core of his political parties.[228]

Dilipak has also published pieces in the newspaper *Yeni Şafak* (New Dawn).[229] Currently he writes for the newspaper *Yeni Akit* (New Contract), which expresses Islamist views and ideas and, along with the television channel *Akit TV*, it belongs to the homonymous group of companies *(Akit Medya Grubu)*. Dilipak is the author of more than sixty books,[230] the majority of which address issues related to Islam, the Islamist movement, the Middle East, politics, society, and ideology in modern Turkey, as well as world history.[231]

Dilipak's Political Activity

Dilipak regards himself as a strict Muslim of the Hanafi school,[232] and it is through this lens that he observes things, reflects, and produces his writings. For approximately two years (1978–1980), he was an active member of Necmettin Erbakan's National Order Party *(Milli Nizam Partisi)*. Dilipak explains that he engaged himself "in active politics only during the period 1978–1980," as at that time he thought that "he had to support the political struggle for faith and identity." In his own words:

> I became a [party] candidate, when they could not find any other candidates. But I did not have the mindset of a politician, I was a citizen. Apart from the National Order Party, I have become no other party's candidate. I had an overall interest in politics, but not as a politician. And I never distanced myself from politics. And I was never part of

---

228 For more information about the structure and ideology of the National View movement, both in Turkey and in Germany, see Konstantinos Gogos, *Turkish Political Islam*, 140–59 and 345–85.

229 See Sena Karasipahi, *Muslims in Modern Turkey: Kemalism, Modernism and the Revolt of the Islamic Intellectuals* (London: I. B. Tauris, 2009), 56.

230 See "Veysel Tepeli'nin Abdurrahman Dilipak-ile-yaptığı Röportaj." As mentioned by Dilipak himself, some of his books have been translated into Arabic, Persian, English, and German.

231 See for example the following titles: *Terörizm* (Terrorism), *Orta Afrika Dosyası* (Central Africa File), *Filistin'de Bir Çocuk* (A Child in Palestine), *Türkiye Nereye Gidiyor?* (Where is Turkey Heading?), *Bir Başka Açıdan Kemalizm* (Kemalism From Another Point of View), *Körfez Savaşı* (The Gulf War), *İnsanlığın Tarihi* (History of Humanity), *İnönü Dönemi* (The Era of İnönü), *Laisizm* (Secularism), *Sorunlar, Sorular ve Cevaplar 1* (Issues, Questions and Answers 1).

232 See "Veysel Tepeli'nin Abdurrahman Dilipak-ile-yaptığı Röportaj."

a political structure, apart from the National Order Party, with which I had ties and a professional relationship during the years 1978–1980.[233]

Dilipak's engagement with the Islamist party of Erbakan came to an end with the military coup of 1980 (12 September), when the Turkish military took power, dissolved Parliament, banned political parties, and arrested party leaders.[234]

As will be illustrated in the following pages, during the past years Dilipak has been supportive of Recep Tayyip Erdoğan and the policies of the Justice and Development Party (JDP). This becomes particularly clear in his writings and speeches about the community of Fethullah Gülen, JDP's foreign policy, or the Palestinian issue and the relations between Turkey and Israel.

Dilipak's Islamist thought

As already mentioned, Dilipak is seen as one of the prominent figures of the Islamist movement in Turkey, who "starting from the premise that Islam is encircled by Western imperialism, supports the prevalence of the political activities of Islamic movements in order to lay the necessary conditions for the development of Islamic society and of Muslim individuals."[235]

Dilipak is one of the chief editors and leading columnists of the Islamist newspaper *Yeni Akit*, which supports Recep Tayyip Erdoğan and the JDP government and criticizes fiercely those whom it regards as enemies of Erdoğan's government, Turkey, and Islam. In other words, *Yeni Akit* denounces politicians and opposition parties, intellectuals, and writers who criticize or oppose the politics of Turkey's government. In addition, minority groups in Turkey, the Western states, Fethullah Gülen with his community and followers, as well as various non-Islamic and democratic social groups and civil society organizations are included among its targets.

Dilipak expresses himself inimically against Jews and the Freemasons, whom he blames for the troubles and maladies that Turkey, the Middle East, and the world are going through. Dilipak's antisemitism is strong and comparable to

---

233 Ibid. He also underlines (again) the following: "Since 1980 I have never had any political commitment. You cannot make a politician out of me. They reside far away from me and I myself reside far away from them. I am a citizen, not a politician."

234 See Erik J. Zürcher, *Turkey: A Modern History* (3rd ed. London – New York: I.B. Tauris, 2010), 278–79.

235 Nilüfer Göle, *The Forbidden Modern*, 110.

the antisemitic stance of Kısakürek. In a relevant text which bears the title "The Hidden Governing Hands"[236] (*Yönetimde Gizli Eller*) he writes the following:

> In Turkey since a long time ago, moreover after the Tanzimat era, during the last years of the Ottomans, masons have been always playing an active role.
>
> The Committee of Union and Progress was a masonic movement. The edict of Tanzimat was masonic as well. We even had sultans and sheikh-ul-islams who were masons.
>
> (...) Let's make clear right away that among the governments of the Turkish Republic there was not a single Council of Ministers without masons. During the single-party period, during the Democratic Party years, as well as in the government which was formed after the DP was overthrown by the coup of 27 May [1960], the prominence of those circles within the [power] structures remained intact. What is interesting to note is that seven out of ten members of the governments that were formed in every urgent situation were masons.

In the same text, he concludes the following:

> (...) one should wonder why mystical Islamic orders in Turkey are stigmatized as a religious reaction[237] and are persecuted, whereas masonic organizations, immoral brotherhoods and activities of Christian missionaries are allowed? [One should wonder] also to which direction do they want Turkey to be led.[238]

Yeni Akit replaced the newspaper *Anadolu'da Vakit* (Time in Anatolia) in 2010, which in turn had replaced the newspaper *Akit* (Contract) in 2001. The latter had been founded in 1993. At this point, it should be said that, according to reliable and recent research,[239] both *Yeni Akit* and *Milli Gazete* occupy the first two places among all publications in the Turkish Press in terms of the rhetoric of hatred and negative prejudices reflected in their pages.[240]

---

236 Abdurrahman Dilipak, *Türkiye Nereye Gidiyor?* (6th ed., Istanbul: Risâle Yayınları, 1989), 128.

237 In Turkish: *irtica*. He means their suppression by the Kemalist secular regime.

238 Abdurrahman Dilipak, *Türkiye Nereye*, 131.

239 See for example the research and reports of the Hrant Dink Foundation (*Hrant Dink Vakfı*), under the title "Medyada Nefret Söylemi ve Ayrımcı Dil" (Rhetoric of Hatred and Discriminatory Language in the Media). For the report of September-December 2014, see Hrant Dink Foundation, *Medyada Nefret Söylemi ve Ayrımcı Dil: Eylül-Aralık 2014 Raporu*, http://nefretsoylemi.org/rapor/EylulAralik2014raporuson.pdf (accessed December 30, 2015).

240 As recorded in the respective reports, the groups that are particularly targeted are the following: Jews, Christians, Armenians, Rum, Kurds, Alevi, Western societies and Western states (in general), British, refugees from Syria (non-Muslim refugees from Syria, Kurdish refugees from Syria), non-Muslims in general, atheists, etc. See "Medyada nefret bilançosu: Yeni Akit zirvede, Yahudiler hedefte!" *Diken*, December

Dilipak managed to cause turmoil at the end of 2014 when he spoke about the necessity of the establishment of an Islamic caliphate at the present time.[241] More concretely, he expressed the need for establishment of the caliphate in Turkey as an institution independent from the state and with ecumenical resonance, which would have for Muslims a role similar to that of the Vatican for the Catholic Church. Dilipak added that the caliph would be elected and that such an institution would not undermine democracy, neither would it harm Turkey's secular character, but on the contrary it would strengthen democracy.[242] Interestingly, in his speech held in Toronto at the end of 2015, he mentioned the following:[243]

> The caliphate has not been abolished, it has just been transferred to the Grand National Assembly of Turkey. Which means that the government will restore it to its rightful position. If Tayyip Erdoğan moves to the presidential system, he will then be nominated in this sense in all cities, in all regions that are dedicated to the caliphate, most probably he will be indicated by special advisors, and the Islamic Union[244] will open representations in Beştepe.[245]

Taking into account Dilipak's influence on religious and Islamist circles, it should be no surprise if this stance is adopted or expressed also by leading members of the JDP or the government in Turkey.

Dilipak's Writings

In the following pages, some representative samples of Dilipak's Islamist thought are quoted. In some cases, the title of the text has been created by myself with the aim of presenting the core of the issue dealt with by Dilipak—although very often the various topics and references of Dilipak cannot be easily isolated or distinguished from each other.

30, 2014, http://www.diken.com.tr/medyada-nefret-bilancosu-yeni-akit-zirvede-yahudiler-hedefte/ (accessed December 30, 2015).

241 See "*Akit* Yazarı Dilipak'tan Hilafet Çağrısı" (Akit's Writer, Dilipak, calls for a Caliphate), *soL*, November 2, 2014, http://haber.sol.org.tr/devlet-ve-siyaset/akit-yazari-dilipaktan-hilafet-cagrisi-haberi-99492 (accessed May 8, 2015).

242 Ibid.

243 See "Dilipak: Erdoğan Başkan Seçilirse Halife Olacak" (Dilipak: If Erdoğan is elected President, he will become Caliph), *Yeni Akit*, October 25, 2015, http://www.yeniakit.com.tr/haber/dilipak-erdogan-baskan-secilirse-halife-olacak-102307.html (accessed March 30, 2016).

244 Dilipak means the Organization of Islamic Cooperation.

245 He refers to the Presidential palace. This is the name of the Ankara district where the new Presidential palace was built by Erdoğan.

Text: "The Three Modes of Politics in the Relationships between Religion and State (Secularism, Theocracy, and Byzantinism)"[246]

The practical application of the relationships between religion and state, as these are widespread, can be placed under one of the following three titles:

a) Secularism (Laiklik): In very broad terms, it means that religion and state are two separate entities.
b) Theocracy (Teokrasi): Religious state.
c) Byzantinism (Bizantinizm): State power over religion.

This distinction may explain Christianity and the Western world. However, in any Islamic society, these words, with their contemporary encyclopedic definitions, fail to explain the existing relationships or the relationships that should exist.

And again, it will not be any easy at all to classify the existing regime in Turkey under any of these definitions. If you look at the Constitution and the [official] documents, Turkey is a secular state. But, in fact, existing practices in Turkey show that there is no alignment with the perception of the secular state in Western terms. In a secular state, by no means can an institution of religious affairs form part of the bureaucracy, as in Turkey. Or, even, the state does not plan to degenerate people's faith while hiding behind compulsory religious courses. Imams are not civil servants. (...)

What is actually being applied in Turkey cannot be explained with [the term] theocracy either. Because religion, regardless of worship and dogma, has been isolated from economic, social, and political life. If someone supports something like this [i.e. theocracy], there will be penal consequences.

However, the regime shows theocratic characteristics as well, in many aspects. If someone looks at the dictionaries of the Turkish Language Institution before 1950, here is what is mentioned: "Kemalism is the religion of the Turks". This is how the entry "religion" is defined. According to the opinion of these circles, Islam is an "Arabic ideology". [They] actually say: "Let Kaaba belong to the Arabs; Çankaya is sufficient for us"[247] while they try to put forward the idea that "*Anıtkabir* is our *kibla*."[248]

Kemalism, the principles and the reforms of Atatürk, are like a religion. Society cannot change them. Atatürk is protected by law. The President of the Republic and the Members of the Parliament take an oath that they will remain faithful to the principles and reforms of Atatürk. Atatürk is a value to which they swear an oath. Devotion to Atatürk is a duty for every patriot. Civil servants, students, and especially the military will undertake any necessary mission in order to remain faithful to these principles,

246 Abdurrahman Dilipak, *Laisizm*, 53–55.
247 He refers to the Presidential House in Ankara, where the President of the Turkish Republic used to live for several decades, until the new Presidential palace was built.
248 *Kibla* is the point in the interior of a mosque showing the direction of Mecca. *Anıtkabir* is the mausoleum of Mustafa Kemal Atatürk, the construction of which was completed in 1953.

to guard and protect the foundations of the state against those who dare to alter these principles.

If Kemalism is indeed a religion (in the name of which reforms are made and *mevlut*[249] poems are written) and if the entry 'religion' in the dictionary of the Turkish Language Institution of the year 1946 is true, we can talk about a Kemalist theocracy in Turkey. From this point of view, Kemalism is not a religion of ethics, philosophy and heaven, it is a religion of civilization. (...)

The practices that currently take place in Turkey show us that the regime has a Byzantinistic character to a larger extent than being secular or theocratic. In other words, the state exercises power over religion. If someone looks at the minutes of the secret meetings of the Grand National Assembly of Turkey, [one will note that] there have been discussions even about the removal from the Holy Quran of the civil verses, the legal verses, with the argument that they are against secularism, and about their replacement with quotes from the *Nutuk*.[250] In this way, what Islamic religion stipulates for daily life is incriminated. According to Aytunç Altındal[251] (see Milliyet, 4 November 1990, p. 5, interview with Özcan Ercan): "Between the perception of secularism in Turkey and the perceptions of secularism and atheism in Western Europe, even in the Soviet Union, there is a huge difference. In my opinion, there is no secularism in Western Europe with the identity and the characteristics of the secularism that exists in Turkey. We are the only country on this track." Maybe it can be described as follows: Byzantinistic theocratic secularism. Fully tailored to us. Maybe it is not clear what this exactly means, however I think that it is a very suitable definition for our situation.

Text: About Islam, Faith and the Human Mind[252]

(...) The religion we believe in defines the earth, sky, death, and life... But the religion we experience does not define anything directly... We either get lost in the foggy sea of the

---

249 *Mevlut* or *mevlid* or *mawlid*: Prophet Muhammad's birth and the celebration of this day, which started being celebrated centuries later. Poems for birthday celebrations are also called *mevlut*.
250 Mustafa Kemal's speech during the second conference of the Republican People's Party, which ook place in the Grand National Assembly of Turkey. The Nutuk speech lasted 36.5 hours, spread throughout six consecutive days (15–20 October 1927). The Nutuk speech has been translated and commented in Greek by Dr. Maro Mavropoulou. See Gazi Mustafa Kemal, *Nutuk*, transl. Maro Mavropoulou, Athens: Papazisis, 2009 (2 volumes).
251 Aytunç Altındal (1945–2013): Publisher and author of books with themes related to history of religions, society, secularism, freemasonry and relevant topics.
252 This title was created by me. The following text comes from the preface of Abdurrahman Dilipak's book *Sorunlar, Sorular ve Cevaplar* (Istanbul: Beyan Yayınları, 1995), 7–12. Some parts of the preface are being quoted here.

past or we become atomic dust in the universe within the uncertainty of the future... We are obliged to create the present-day anew, with the accumulated knowledge of the past and hope for the future... While times change, knowledge that has no divine origin will also change, judgments will also change. However, the revelation will not change, but, because we change ourselves, our understanding of the revelation will evolve towards the same direction as well. Because we believe as far as our mind can reach, we can act as far as our mind can reach...[253]

(...) [To put it] more clearly, we did not attempt to give people ready fish. We wanted to teach people how to fish. As Confucius said, if you give people a fish, then you feed them for a day, if you give them a fish every day, you let them get addicted to begging, if you teach them how to fish, then they will be able to fill their stomach with their labor and dignity.[254]

(...) For this reason, I am telling you not to rent out your mind... In fact, because I do not answer every question that I am asked, sometimes confusion is caused in people's mind. I think that I fulfill my duty by letting people know what they do not know, by loading them down with the pain of searching for the truth... The most important knowledge [for someone] is the awareness of [his/her] ignorance and the right question will definitely find its answer...[255]

(...) Just as the mill does not turn if no water falls, one can also not become a scientist with the knowledge one has heard by oneself, [in the same way] religion is not being learned...[256]

We will get to know our religion, and the safest way for this is studying. Afterwards we will reflect on what we read, and through discussion and advice we will check if we understood correctly or not. Afterwards we will act accordingly and we will test in practice the conclusions we reached. We will announce to people the results we reached... And if there are any obstacles to living in this way, or if attempts are made to prevent this announcement, we will fight against them... Or, moreover, we will wage jihad in order to make people aware of these truths...

(...) It is necessary to not forget that the thought of a moment is more beneficial than the prayers of thousands of years... We believe and we act as far as our mind allows us [to do so], but the mind itself is neither the source nor the measure of truth... I actually believe that even with regard to our problems we should not be pushed to the limits of this measure...[257]

(...) The mind by itself can cause disaster in the name of salvation. We should not forget that Satan is the first one to reflect... The ways to hell are paved with stones of good intentions... And Satan uses the mind. To believe means to accept...

---

253 Ibid., 8.
254 Ibid., 9.
255 Ibid.
256 Ibid., 9–10.
257 Ibid., 10.

(...) We should know that our mind is not the source and measure of truth and that the mind has limits... We should think anew that we accept the existence of one single creator. Religion is the life guide that the creator revealed to his creations and [also] the knowledge of truth. It expresses the will of God who created the mind. Religion is the knowledge of truth...[258]

Text: On the Dominance of Muslims[259]

(...) When a new era rises, in such times, it is our obligation to understand, to express and to experience Islam through its own sources.

Within the future revolutions, the loudest voice will be that of Islam... And this enhances our responsibilities. (...) If we neglect to fulfill our duty, [then] the cost and the risk of this affair will be extremely high... We may smelt under the problems that come along with the new era and we may miss one more opportunity... I hope that this will not happen... In a period of time when communism has collapsed, [a period] which is captured by capitalism, rising Islam opens a new door of hope regarding the future of humanity.

It is not Islam that will come. It is the Muslims... One thousand five hundred years have passed since Islam arrived. Neither a new religion will come nor a new holy book nor a new prophet... We are the ones to come... And for this reason, we have to deploy and thicken our lines... Those who believe in God, in his Prophet, in his Book, while being conscious of the fact that they are one single community, have to revert to God for their issues, to his Prophet and his Book and, instead of rectifying their religion according to their organizations and their leaders, they have to get together in the contract with God, evaluating their leaders and their organizations according to the Quran... They have to call the people, not to their leaders, their organizations and their ideologies, but to God and his Prophet. (...) We have to be again martyrs of our religion... We have to truly know what we claim to believe in.[260]

Text: "Is Democracy a Form of Islamic Governance?"

The following text is part of a longer answer that Dilipak gave to the question of whether democracy is a form of Islamic governance. At the end of the text, Dilipak states that he is in favor of the "social order of Medina" (*Medine toplum düzeni*). It is clear that Dilipak agrees with Bulaç on the significance of the "social order of Medina" and its role as a model for the contemporary social, political, and judicial organization of Muslim societies and states.

---

258 Ibid., 10–11.
259 This title was created by me.
260 Abdurrahman Dilipak, *Sorunlar, Sorular,* 11–12.

(...) We need to examine democracy (*demokrasi*) in detail, on the basis of its conceptual foundations and its historical development.

Let me clarify right away the following: in my opinion, the main difference between democracy and Islam is that Islam is the product of religion, whereas democracy is the product of ideology, [the product] of an idea. The former promises felicity in this world and pledges paradise. The latter promises in this world paradise... In other words, the sources of democracy are not divine, its methods are not Islamic, and its goals are not the will of God (*Allah*)...

Since all beautiful things are within Islam, some people starting from the thought that in democracy there are beautiful values as well enter strange paths searching either for an Islamic democracy or for Islam in democracy... In my view, this does no justice either to Islam or to democracy. Each and every single thing has a value and a meaning within its own logic and its own totality... The attempt to describe or define a thing in a different way is a sign of weakness. Islam does not accept weakness though.

I am afraid that, even when we define our religion, we do not rely on its own sources, but we perceive it through the habits of our ancestors and through the ideologies that prevail nowadays in our world... By using Islam as a means, we want to come closer to what capitalism, socialism, democracy, and secularism promise. . . For this reason, we often opt for the way of synthesis... Islam appears in front of us as an additional ingredient, as a complementary element... However, Islam, having nothing more and nothing less, is a guide for life which the creator revealed to [his] creation.

Without doubt, from this, one should not conclude that I reject certain things, [and the] high values which democracy, socialism, and secularism pledge... While saying this, we should not make the mistake and, from the idea that "there is no coercion in religion", end up at secularism. In addition, from socialism and communism we should not end up at sovietism and communitarianism, nor should we interpret the power with which we are administered according to the democracy we are in...

As there will be no Turkish-Islamic synthesis, i.e. as religion will never be able to be synthesized with races, leaders, schools, it cannot be synthesized with ideologies either... If a Marxist or a monk demonstrates some elements which characterize a Muslim, this does not mean that he is also a Muslim.

Democracy is a system which secularizes the person, on the basis of human, rather than divine, will... Source and measure of truth is not the divine will but the human mind. Religion is a system of faith and it expresses a field which is related to future life. Religion is a field that the person finds in his own self while searching for the unknown, the eternal and the nonperishable. Nobody can meddle in this. The church on the other hand is the castle of religion. It expresses the earthly dimension of divine will. Secularism is the fact of truce and definition of the dividing line between God (*Tanrı*) and the King (*Kral*) in the West. Render unto Caesar the things that are Caesar's, and unto God the things that are God's...[261]

---

261 Ibid., 84–86.

Dilipak further explains:

(...) Besides, Western thinkers do not define democracy as the best possible form of governance, but as the less harmful system or as a system which is regarded to be best among the worst... But to us democracy – without being based on any intellectual foundation at all – appears like a benevolent prayer, like a vague hope which was given to desperate people...

Look at the experience of contemporary Western democracy, which appeared for the first time with the French revolution in 1789. Look at its cost... Two World Wars, air, water, and soil pollution, the atomic bomb explosions in Nagasaki and Hiroshima... Exhaustion of raw material resources, wars, hunger, poverty... Democracy is a source of happiness for a happy minority of five hundred million [people], who live on the one sixth [of the surface] of the earth. But if they happen to share this happiness with other countries, the prosperity and happiness of the West will be much more limited... This is why Western democracies show a nationalist, defensive and conservative character. They [Westerners] need to have second class democracies for their democracies. In the hands of the Westerners, democracy means no more than a beauty masque, a charming amulet. Take the example of the coup d'état in Algeria, take the example of the puppet governments and collaborator regimes in the Arabian Peninsula.

Since the source and measure of truth was the human mind, then the mind of which human being was this at all?... You see, capitalism, communism, and fascism were born out of the different answers that were given to this question... All three of them were very tightly connected to the principles of rationalism, determinism, and pragmatism, principles that constitute the three fundamental proclamations of the religion of democracy... They examined the facts and the things with a rationalist, utilitarian, and causal logic... Besides, the Encyclopedists were anew commenting on and redefining everything with the same logic... According to fascism, the human being who was the source and measure of truth was the human being of the German race. Everything would be organized anew for the Germans, by the Germans and according to the Germans... Hitler, who fought against the Jews, was re-examining the truth using the Judaic logic, using exactly the theory of racial superiority of the Jews. .. As "Führer", leader of the German race, he would become himself the god of all gods... Without any doubt, it was the expression of a disease which we can call "Pharaoh syndrome" ... This adventure, which cost the life of millions of people, did not last long. According to communism, on the other hand, the source and measure of truth was the right of the worker, the right of the one who possesses the labor, possesses the goods, produces the goods. Communism also came to an end, leaving behind hundreds of millions of dead, blood and tears... The Kremlin was the *kibla* of the new religion of atheism. The general secretary of the party was the god of all gods... The [members of the] presidium [were] the saints and the apostles of this new religion... The members of the party [were] like young monks and nuns, the heads of the communes [were] like communist eremites. The superior race was the working class. Everything was done by the workers, for the workers and according to the workers...

Capitalism, the third out of the three bastard children of this democracy, on the issue of the source and measure of truth, was thinking exactly like a Jew... Who has the power and the strength will prevail... Strong is the one who has wealth, weapons, and power. Since money is the symbol of power, whoever has more money, will set the rules and the world will be formed according to his will...

Capitalism is still shedding blood... America claims the status of lord and god... It restores and destroys, in a demonstration of power... It claims to be the pole of the world... It wants to give the world a new order... Those who attach themselves to the tail of America are like the female servants who want to sit at the table of gods... America is the new Zeus.

Democracy is the political tool of liberalism... And liberalism is like the social and economic tool of democracy... Whereas in the economy the natural result of liberalism is capitalism. All these should have nothing to do with Islam. Or, in other words, from an Islamic point of view these cannot be evaluated as positive things in any case.

Democracy functions like a Trojan horse for Western cultural imperialism. The aim is to market this Judeo-Greek culture (*Judeo-Grek kültürü*) to Islamic countries in a democracy package.

Islam promises much more than democracy. Democracy is a construction which suppresses and limits me. Without doubt, I am not really interested if someone is a leftist, a Christian, or a democrat. Even if someone is a democrat I am not bothered, I can even co-sign most of his demands, which are raised in the name of democracy, but I am not a democrat. This again does not mean that I am an enemy of democracy. However, I am not a democrat... This concept is not sufficient to express my fears and hopes, my emotions and thoughts. It does not explain to me how we will go to paradise, which is the real reason of living in this world. And perhaps I can use such a political chewing gum, like everybody does, but this will be disrespectful towards myself and the democrats as well... Their democracy to them, my religion to me.

I think that many of those who regard themselves as democrats know neither what democracy means nor what the difference between democracy (*demokrasi*) and republic (*cumhuriyet*) is.

I am not so sure that they know the mere lexicological equivalent of democracy... As exactly they do not know these, they also do not know that they do not know. And this is the result of our multilayered ignorance... The most obvious qualification of the systemic ignorant people that these schools have raised is that they believe that they know, although they don't know...

If we analyze democracy as a word, it consists of the words Demos and Kratos, that is, two words which mean something like governance of people. On the issue of governance there is no dispute, but on the issue who is the Demos, i.e. how people are defined, there is a dispute already since a long time... If you write down your own name in the place of Demos, [then] in this sense everyone becomes a democrat... In ancient Greece, i.e. in the first prototype of democracy, Demos referred to male nobles... Slaves and women were not included in the notion of people and only male nobles had the right to vote... In other words, women and slaves had no place in Greek democracy.

Of course, another interesting aspect of the matter is that those who view the one-thousand-five-hundred-year-old Islam as an old order [of things], stick to a five-thousand-year-old term such as democracy... As if there are some things that never get old. But probably it shouldn't be such an easy task to explain this to them.

In communist countries, Demos were the people... Or, in theocratic regimes, Demos are the priests. In capitalist countries, Demos are those who possess the wealth. For feminists, Demos means most probably the female population.

As far as the second part of the question is concerned, [namely if] various organizations can exist within the Islamic society? [If] it is possible to found parties? Actually, the background of this question has nothing to do with Islamic concerns... It seems like a claim to incorporate Islam in other systems, to discover the world that they pledge on the name of Islam.

Today in the modern world, national and geographical federations are under consideration. I advocate an idea which takes as a basis the social order of Medina[262].[263]

About the Method of Islamic Struggle

The following passage is part of Dilipak's reply to a question about the appropriate "method of Islamic struggle,"[264] in other words, which method the Islamist movement needs to follow in Turkey in order to achieve its goals. It should be noted that he refers to the social and legal order of Medina and its "multi-judicial system" as a model to be applied. A significant part of his text follows:

In the second part of your question, you are asking "how the struggle for the Islamic way of life and for the dominance of Islam in society should be carried out."

As I perceive this, everyone should live according to what he believes, he should not force others to Islam. Following his own right, his own sharia, within the context of a contract which defines the principle of co-existence between [existing] differences, each of us should accept as a basis the provisions of [this] contract as far as relationships towards others are concerned... It is thus a multi-judicial system... We are neither God

262 In Turkish: *Medine toplum düzeni.*
263 Abdurrahman Dilipak, *Sorunlar, Sorular,* 90–95.
264 Dilipak presents the following question: "Under today's circumstances, how should the struggle for the Islamic way of life and the domination of Islam in the society we live in be carried out? With a revolution, like in the case of Iran? With a military coup, like in the case of Pakistan? With democratic methods, like in the case of Algeria? Or, according to different, not yet successful examples, like the case of Syria, where a hidden armed organized fight is taking place, or the method that a group of the [Muslim] Brothers is applying in Egypt, which aims to change the society through proclamations? In your opinion, which method should we take as example?" Abdurrahman Dilipak, *Sorunlar, Sorular,* 96–97.

nor deity of these [others]. And respectively we do not yield to their views about God and the divine. The religion of each person belongs to him/ herself.

On the other hand, for us there is no such dominance issue. We are slaves. The almighty, the absolute ruler and judge is Allah, that is, dominance belongs to Allah... Judgment belongs to Allah. This Allah who, when he sent people to this world, he gave them the freedom to get to know him or not; and, by showing them the truth and the lie, he intro-duced paradise to those who align with the truth, whereas he threatened with hell those who deny it. No matter whether they accept him or not, they are already part of Allah's will. Satan is also part of Allah's will. We claim Allah's consent. (...) I think that Muslims have no issue of dominance over others. I am repeating, judgment belongs to Allah. In this sense, we must not have any issue of dominance.

Coming to the second part of your question: regarding the model – that of Iran, Pakistan, or Algeria? Well, just think for a moment, on which model were these based? Why should we follow a second-hand strategy? In my opinion, we should approach the issue by taking lessons from history... [There is] also the hope for the future... It is neces-sary that we establish the boundaries between yesterday and tomorrow...

In addition, we should also think the following... If this is [to be] a natural change of function, why should we revolt saying that it is a coup d'état or a revolution? With the weapons of our opponents... I believe that we should fight with the same [means] with which they come upon us. This is something related to the circumstances... As time, space, and circumstances change, [our] judgment will change as well... Undoubtedly, we are obliged to take lessons from the experiences of Iran, Pakistan, Algeria, and the [Muslim] Brothers.

I pay more attention to the process than to a struggle which aims exclusively at the result. Every person should do his share, participate in the community while being conscious of his individual responsibility. I am not referring to a community which is [organized] like a herd... And not everyone has to behave in the same way. I am dreaming of a more pluralistic, polyphonic, and multicultural society... Of course, we will believe in the same thing, as Muslims, but we are not obliged to think of the same thing... It is necessary that we have certain principles, but I do not find it right that this is expressed through a chain of militaristic orders. I do not think that there is one single method that can be applied everywhere... Sometimes with the sword, sometimes through discussions, sometimes by compromising, sometimes with consultations and councils... Following the example of our Prophet. . . Yes, this way. (...)[265]

About the Turkish-Islamic Synthesis

Dilipak rejects the ideological proposal of Turkish-Islamic synthesis (*Türk-İslam Sentezi*), that is, the creation and application of a political-ideological synthesis between Islam and Turkish nationalism, an idea which played an important role

---

265 Ibid., 98–100.

among Turkish intellectuals and in Turkish politics—particularly during the last quarter of the 20th century. In this respect, he writes the following:

> How much do an apple and a pear make? Such a question is of course not possible. . . But if you peel both and you make a fruit salad, then you get an apple-ish pear or a pear-ish apple. (...)
>
> Is it possible for a Turkish-Islamic synthesis to exist? According to some, why not? They actually believe that this is the only way out of the dead end, the only solution [to the problems] ... However, one of them is religion, whereas the other one is a human element... Are we going to use Turkishness for the strengthening of Islam or the inadequacy of Islam or are we going to use Islam as a complementary piece of Turkishness? Without a doubt, none of these two can happen. Because religion cannot accept to have something added or removed. (...)
>
> If such a Turkish-Islamic synthesis could exist, then respectively it will also be possible for an Arabic-Islamic synthesis or an Afghan-Islamic synthesis to exist, which is against the declaration of Islam to make all people brothers and sisters.
>
> The idea of Turkish-Islamic synthesis actually came to the foreground in the 1950s, with the government of the Democratic Party that was against the policy of oppression of Islam, which was implemented during the period of the National Chief,[266] and aimed at the extermination of religion. The goal was to make all Muslims support right-wing policies, and this campaign was successful. [They] claimed that right-wing policies protect the Muslims from the Left, but in order to prevent religious people from expressing their real demands, they were constructing imaginary ideologies for the Muslims.[267]

On the Community of Fethullah Gülen

During the past years, Dilipak has often expressed himself against Gülen, his activities, and his network, while fiercely supporting R.T. Erdoğan and the JDP government. Indicative of his stance and very characteristic of the style of his texts in the press is his article in the newspaper *Yeni Akit*, on 3 November 2014, under the title "Is There Only One Type of *Cemaat*?"[268]

> (...) Within the *Cemaat* there are leftists, social democrats and even leftist democrats. There are also nationalist leftists and socialists...
>
> The *Cemaat* has hidden figures who conceal their real identity, it has a thousand faces...

---

266 İsmet İnönü, the second President of Turkey (November 1938–May 1950), was called "National Chief."

267 Abdurrahman Dilipak, *Türkiye Nereye*, 50–52.

268 *Cemaat* means community and it generally refers to the communities of the Muslim mystical orders. In Turkey, this is the widespread short name for the network of Fethullah Gülen.

The *Cemaat* has strong supporters that are not Muslims. Among those there are Jews, Christians, Catholics, Protestants, Orthodox, members of independent churches, there are people from all fields who cooperate with each other.

It was not Fethullah Gülen who founded the *Cemaat!*[269]

Within the *Cemaat* there are not only teachers, but also army officers, policemen, wardens, clerks, minute takers, court secretaries. There are also doctors and businessmen... As well as engineers and well-known scientists... They can be found everywhere, we are talking about a structure with an age of a quarter of a century... Of course, its roots go back to the 1960s, and its last period is the quarter of the century... Behind this you have the CIA, RAND, Mossad, Masons, Templars, Germans, British, French, everyone... In a way it brings to mind the P2 Lodge...

This structure was not established by Gülen, it is not even directed by him... He is just the man on display... The influence of Hoca Efendi[270] on the command of this structure is equal to the influence of the spokesman of the White House on the formation of the content of his announcements!

A parallel state is not the only problem. In fact, the global reality was founded upon a parallel perception of religion... [What is their aim?] The existence and security of Israel, [and] an ecumenical missionary activity aimed at the spreading in the Muslim world of a parallel new perception of religion, with the reserve of Christianity, squeezed within the system of Western values, Western notions and institutions so that it does not form any danger for the West, imprisoned in the consciousnesses on an individual level, in the temples on a social level, and an Islamic world which does not form any danger for the military and strategic plans of the USA and NATO. This is what they want to accomplish.

In this way, according to this plan, they want to redefine the borders of the Islamic states, the regimes and their structures of power... This is the real essence of the structure called *Cemaat*. And they have to finish this immediately since they want to finish the job before the ninety-nine-year period of certain privileged agreements comes to an end.

Since they saw the AKP[271] and the İHH[272] as an obstacle to their own pursuits, they unleashed an attack against these organizations... However, earlier they were supporting

---

269 The emphasis in the sentence as in the original text.

270 i.e. Fethullah Gülen.

271 The Justice and Development Party. In Turkish: *Adalet ve Kalkınma Partisi* (AKP).

272 Dilipak means the Turkish Islamic non-governmental organization İHH-*İnsan Hak ve Hürriyetleri İnsani Yardım Vakfı* (The Foundation for Human Rights and Freedoms and Humanitarian Relief) which has its head office in Istanbul and is active in many countries and places throughout the world, with its recipients being mainly Muslim groups. This organization owns the ship *Mavi Marmara*, which was leading the fleet that tried to break the blockade of Gaza in May 2010, causing the intervention of the armed forces of Israel, which resulted in the death of nine passengers of the ship and injury of dozen others. This incident instigated a significant rupture in the relationships between Israel and Turkey.

AKP with the aim to organize the political network of this matter within their own structures. They would create the political network of the parallel structure [of the plan] BOP.[273] In order to make Erdoğan toe the line, Baykal would come out in the [Presidential Palace] in Çankaya, whereas the *Cemaat* through bureaucracy and information services would take over the control of power or, more correctly, of Erdoğan. Erdoğan, with his stance in the Mavi Marmara incident and the One Minute incident,[274] spoiled this scenario and initiated a war [against them]. Nevertheless, when the arrival of Baykal in the [Presidential Palace] in Çankaya was hindered, the rope was already cut. Baykal and Kiliçdaroğlu are also within the parallel structure as you will understand... Of course, there are also others...What kind of *Cemaat* would it be, there is no one who is not inside it![275]

Conclusion

The quoted texts are indicative of Abdurrahman Dilipak's thought and views. The reader cannot fail to notice that Dilipak's style of writing and expression is torrential, enthusiastic, direct—especially in his columns. When he deals with a topic in his books, he usually adopts a historical approach and uses his knowledge of history, while, in order to support his arguments, he also employs knowledge of sociology and political sciences. However, sometimes in his analysis it is possible to come across inaccuracies or mistakes, especially in topics related to the West and its history (these can be noticed by a careful and informed reader) though it does not deprive Dilipak's work of its overall significance.

The argument that Dilipak expresses the political trend of the Islamist movement—or else, political Islamism—can be confirmed. With regard to his ideas and views, Dilipak is actually characterized by a remarkable diachronical stability.

---

273 i.e. Büyük Orta Doğu Projesi (BOP). This is the Turkish equivalent of the "Great Middle East Project".

274 Dilipak refers to the incident between the Prime Minister of Turkey, Erdoğan, on the one hand, and the President of Israel Shimon Peres and the coordinator of the discussion, on the other hand, which took place in Davos on January 29, 2009. During the discussion on the topic of the attack of Israel in Gaza, Erdoğan said at one point "one minute" demanding that more time be given to express himself. After accusing Israel and Peres in a strict tone, he walked out of the panel discussion. Ever since, the incident in question and the expression "one minute" became very popular in Turkey.

275 Abdurrahman Dilipak, "Cemaat tek tip mi?" *Yeni Akit*, November 3, 2014, http://www.yeniakit.com.tr/yazarlar/abdurrahman-dilipak/cemaat-tek-tip-mi-8308.html (accessed December 30, 2015).

Dilipak differs from Bulaç in certain fundamental points. More concretely, Dilipak places special emphasis on the political activism of Muslims for the realization of an authentic, prosperous Islamic society. In this context though, he prioritizes Turkish identity, Turkish society, and the Turkish nation and state. For Dilipak, a worldwide Muslim society which will be above national borders and national identities is not a priority. With regard to these two points, i.e. political activism and Turco-centrism, it is obvious that he has more in common with the Islamist thought of Kısakürek. Kısakürek had ties with political leaders and parties, recognizing their role in the shaping of an Islamic society and polity. Dilipak belongs to the ardent and determined supporters of Erdoğan and his policies, he maintains very good relationships with JDP members, he opposes the opposition and the Gülen community, and he attacks those states and those leaders whom he regards as enemies of Turkey and the Muslim world. His critique and opposition towards the Jews, Freemasons and those who are regarded as their collaborators—an element that characterizes Kısakürek's thought as well—holds a central position in Dilipak's thought. It is clear that his thought expresses and reflects the Islamist bipolar worldview of "Islam vs. Non-Islam," which targets those regarded enemies of Islam and the Muslim world.

In recent years, i.e. the years of the JDP's government, Dilipak's support towards Erdoğan and his policies has been obvious and dominant. He is an engaged Islamist writer with concrete ideas and views, who fights for the success of Erdoğan and the JDP, and for the strengthening of the Islamic identity in Turkey. He is fiercely opposed to Gülen, his community and his supporters. Regarding this topic, he is obviously an opponent of Bulaç. On the other side, he agrees with Bulaç on the importance of the first social and legal organization of Medina as a model for the social order that Muslim societies should follow in present times.

Furthermore, additional to the influence that Dilipak exercises on his readers and audience, the impact of his ideas on JDP politicians and within Turkish political Islam is important—and this gives more value and practical usefulness to the study and knowledge of his thought and writings.

Epilogue

In the previous chapters, my intention has been to familiarize the reader with the writings and ideas of three prolific Turkish Islamist intellectuals and writers. These intellectuals have highly influenced not only the Turkish Islamist movement itself, but also their readership and many politicians in Turkey during the second half of the 20th century (most significantly during the last quarter of the century) and the first two decades of the 21st century. An attempt has made to shed light on the common ideological and theoretical starting points, as well as the differences regarding the imperatives and priorities of the three writers in question. It is worth noting that the writings and ideas of the specific Islamist intellectuals remain almost unknown outside Turkey—even in countries with a long tradition in Turkish and Islamic studies and research.

Ali Bulaç and Abdurrahman Dilipak are present-day Islamist writers. However, their thought has been influenced not only by the thought of previous Islamist intellectuals, but also by the economic, political, and social changes that have taken place in Turkey and the world since the last decades of the 20th century. As Islamist writers they share some common characteristics; though, as already stressed by prominent scholars, it could be said that Bulaç places more emphasis on the cultural dimension of the Islamist movement, whereas Dilipak emphasizes the political. Nevertheless, it should be noted (and repeated) that both of them are, in essence, Islamist, since both of these dimensions serve, ultimately, the same goals; namely political change and the organization of society and the state according to the imperatives of Islam. Moreover, it should be always kept in mind that the political/cultural distinction is not a clear-cut line, since in the writings and ideas of these two writers (as well as others) the political and cultural aspects of the Islamist movement are obviously and very frequently intertwined and impossible to separate from one another.

As characteristic and significant representatives of the current generations of Turkish Islamist writers, both Bulaç and Dilipak have been influenced by the thought and action of Necip Fazıl Kısakürek, although they are not characterized by Kısakürek's philosophical and deep mystical background. Kısakürek functions as a link between the Islamists of the late Ottoman Empire and the Islamists that emerged during the last quarter of the twentieth century. Beyond his undoubtedly rare literary and poetical talent, it can be argued that he is not just an Islamist writer, but an Islamist ideologist with theoretical and practical work. It can also be noted that his ideas and thought combine the cultural and political dimensions of the Islamist movement together with (Turkish) nationalism. These elements constitute the ideological bridge that led from Ottoman Islamist thought to the present-day Turkish Islamist thought and intelligentsia—and have also exercised influence over the Turkish nationalist thought.

In a broader sense, this study seeks to contribute to the knowledge and understanding of the trends of Islamist thought in contemporary Turkey, by presenting original writings which reveal certain ideological stances and perceptions that occupy a dominant position in modern Turkish society, and influence a significant part of the educated conservative Muslim readership. In practice, this can be useful in order to understand the hegemonic position of the Justice and Development Party, as well as the struggle between different poles of the Turkish Islamist movement. And, if we go one step further, it leads us to further questions regarding the future of the Islamist movement in Turkey, and regarding the Islamizing or Islamist trends in the society and governance of Turkey.

This book is not to be seen as an exhaustive study of contemporary Turkish Islamist writings; it has the humble ambition to encourage further academic research on this topic. Further research on Turkish Islamist thought and writings may prove to be particularly fruitful and useful for the study and understanding of the trajectory and the dimensions of the Turkish Islamist movement; it can substantially contribute to the comparative study of the Islamist movement and Islamist thought in Turkey, in other countries of the Middle East, and in the Muslim world in general.

Needless to say, it is the reader who will judge whether this book has fulfilled my intention and its purpose.

Bibliography

Reference Works

Philosophy Lexicon [in Greek: Λεξικόν της Φιλοσοφίας]. Edited by Theodosis Pelegrinis. New enriched ed. Athens: Pedio, 2013.

The Blackwell Dictionary of Modern Social Thought. Edited by William Outhwaite. 2nd ed. Oxford: Blackwell Publishing, 2003.

The Encyclopedia of Philosophy. Editor in Chief: Paul Edwards. Reprint ed. New York: Macmillan, 1972.

The Oxford Companion to Philosophy. Edited by Ted Honderich. Oxford: Oxford University Press, 1995.

Books, Dissertations, Monographs, and Articles

Abadan-Unat, Nermin. "Ideologische Strömungen in der Türkei in den 90er Jahren." *Südosteuropa Mitteilungen* 4 (1997): 291–300.

Aydın, Cemil. "Between Occidentalism and the Global Left: Islamist Critiques of the West in Turkey." *Comparative Studies of South Asia, Africa and the Middle East*, 26:3 (2006): 446–61.

Berkes, Niyazi. *The Development of Secularism in Turkey*. With a new introduction by Feroz Ahmad. New York: Routledge, 1998.

Bostan Ünsal, Fatma and Ertan Özensel. "Ali Bulaç." In *İslamcılık*. Vol. 6 of Modern Türkiye'de Siyasi Düşünce. Edited by Yasin Aktay, 736–57. Istanbul: İletişim Yayınları, 2004.

Bourdieu, Pierre. *The Field of Cultural Production: Essays on Art and Literature*. Cambridge: Polity Press, 1993.

Bourdieu, Pierre. "Social Space and Symbolic Power." *Sociological Theory* 7:1 (Spring 1989): 14–25.

Bourdieu, Pierre. *Raisons pratiques: Sur la théorie de l'action*. Paris: Éditions du Seuil, 1994.

Bourdieu, Pierre. "The Forms of Capital". In *Readings in Economic Sociology*. Edited by Nicole Woolsey Biggart, 280–91. Oxford: Blackwell Publishers, 2002.

Bulaç, Ali. *Çağdaş Kavramlar ve Düzenler*. 20th edition. Istanbul: İz Yayıncılık, 2007.

Bulaç, Ali. *İslam ve Fundamentalizm*. Istanbul: İz Yayıncılık, 1997.

Bulaç, Ali. "İslam'ın Üç Siyaset Tarzı veya İslamcıların Üç Nesli." In *İslamcılık.* Vol. 6 of Modern Türkiye'de Siyasi Düşünce. Edited by Yasin Aktay, 48–67. Istanbul: İletişim Yayınları, 2004.

Bulaç, Ali. *Modern Ulus Devlet.* 2nd edition. Istanbul: İz Yayıncılık, 1998.

Bulaç, Ali. "The Medina Document." In *Liberal Islam: A Sourcebook.* Edited by Charles Kurzman. New York: Oxford University Press, 1998.

Cantek, Levent. "Büyük Doğu." In *Muhafazakârlık.* Vol. 5 of Modern Türkiye'de Siyasi Düşünce. Edited by Ahmet Çiğdem, 645–55. Istanbul: İletişim Yayınları, 2003.

Çınar, Menderes, and Ayşe Kadıoğlu. "An Islamic Critique of Modernity in Turkey: Politics of Difference Backwards." *ORIENT* 40:1 (1999): 53–69.

Davutoglu, Ahmet. *Alternative Paradigms: The Impact of Islamic and Western Weltanschauungs on Political Theory.* Lanham, Maryland: University Press of America, 1994.

Dilipak, Abdurrahman. *Laisizm.* 2nd edition. Istanbul: Beyan Yayınları, 1991.

Dilipak, Abdurrahman. *Sorunlar, Sorular ve Cevaplar.* Istanbul: Beyan Yayınları, 1995.

Dilipak, Abdurrahman. *Türkiye Nereye Gidiyor?* 6th edition. Istanbul: Risâle Yayınları, 1989.

Doğumunun 100. Yılında Necip Fazıl Kısakürek 1904–1983. Istanbul: İstanbul Büyükşehir Kültür Yayınları, n.d.

Duran, Burhanettin. *Transformation of Islamist Political Thought in Turkey from the Empire to the Early Republic (1908–1960): Necip Fazil Kisakürek's Political Ideas.* PhD diss., Bilkent University, Ankara 2001. In http://www.thesis. bilkent.edu. tr/0001603.pdf

Eickelman, Dale F. "Clash of Cultures? Intellectuals, their publics, and Islam". In *Intellectuals in the Modern Islamic World: Transmission, Transformation, Communication.* Edited by Stephane A. Dudoignon, Komatsu Hisao, and Kosugi Yasushi, 289–304. London: Routledge, 2006.

Esposito, John L. and John O. Voll. *Makers of Contemporary Islam.* New York: Oxford University Press, 2001.

Gazi Mustafa Kemal, *Nutuk* [in Greek: *Ο Μέγας Ρητορικός*]. Translated by Maro Mavropoulou. Athens: Papazisis, 2009 (2 volumes).

Gogos, Konstantinos. *Turkish Political Islam and Islamist Networks in Germany* [in Greek: *Τουρκικό Πολιτικό Ισλάμ και Ισλαμιστικά Δίκτυα στη Γερμανία*]. Athens: Livanis, 2011.

Gogos, Konstantinos. "Political Islam in the Middle East: A Story of Failure or Success?" [in Greek: "Το Πολιτικό Ισλάμ στη Μέση Ανατολή: Μια Ιστορία Αποτυχίας ή Επιτυχίας;"]. In *Proceedings of the 1st Middle Eastern Conference of the National and Kapodistrian University of Athens: 10–12 December 2012*, edited by Ioannis Mazis and Kyriakos Nikolaou Patragas, 57–69. Athens: Leimon, 2013.

Gogos, Konstantinos. "Turkish Islamist intellectuals and the Islamist movement: the view of Ali Bulaç" [in Greek: "Η Τουρκική Ισλαμιστική Διανόηση και το Ισλαμιστικό Κίνημα: Η Θεώρηση του Ali Bulaç"]. In *Tourkologika*, edited by G. Salakidis, 423–36. Thessaloniki: Ant. Stamoulis, 2011.

Gogos, Konstantinos. "Contemporary Turkish Islamist Intellectuals and the Rise of Political Islam in Turkey" [in Greek: "Η Σύγχρονη Ισλαμική Διανόηση και η Άνοδος του Πολιτικού Ισλάμ στην Τουρκία"]. *Γεωστρατηγική [Geostrategy]* 9 (May–August 2006): 95–105.

Göle, Nilüfer. "Islamic Visibilities and Public Sphere." In *Islam in Public: Turkey, Iran, and Europe*, edited by Nilüfer Göle and Ludwig Amman, 3–43. Istanbul: Istanbul Bilgi University Press, 2006.

Göle, Nilüfer. "Secularism and Islamism in Turkey: The Making of Elites and Counter-Elites." *Middle East Journal* 5:1 (Winter 1997): 46–58.

Göle, Nilüfer. *The Forbidden Modern: Civilization and Veiling*. Ann Arbor: The University of Michigan Press, 1996.

Guida, Michelangelo. "Founders of Islamism in Republican Turkey: Kısakürek and Topçu." In *Intellectuals and Civil Society in the Middle East: Liberalism, Modernity and Political Discourse*, edited by Mohammed A. Bamyeh, 111–32. London: I. B. Tauris, 2012.

Guida, Michelangelo. "The New Islamists' Understanding of Democracy in Turkey: The Examples of Ali Bulaç and Hayreddin Karaman." *Turkish Studies* 11:3 (2010): 347–70.

Hanioğlu, M. Şükrü. *A Brief History of the Late Ottoman Empire*. Princeton: Princeton University Press, 2008.

Kadıoğlu, Ayşe. "Women's Subordination in Turkey: Is Islam Really the Villain?" *Middle East Journal* 48:4 (Autumn 1994): 645–60.

Karasipahi, Sena. *Muslims in Modern Turkey: Kemalism, Modernism and the Revolt of the Islamic Intellectuals*. London: I. B. Tauris, 2009.

Kentel, Ferhat. "1990'ların İslami Düşünce Dergileri ve Yeni Müslüman Entelektüeller." In *İslamcılık*. Vol. 6 of Modern Türkiye'de Siyasi Düşünce. Edited by Yasin Aktay, 721–81. Istanbul: İletişim Yayınları, 2004.

Khosrokhavar, Farhad. "The New Intellectuals in Iran". *Social Compass*, 51:2 (2004): 191–202.

Kısakürek, Necip Fazıl. *İdeolocya Örgüsü*. 21st edition. Istanbul: Büyük Doğu Yayınları, 2014.

Kurzman, Charles and Lynn Owens. "The Sociology of Intellectuals." *Annual Review of Sociology* 28 (2002): 63–90.

Lapidot, Anat. *Islam and Nationalism: A Study of Contemporary Political Thought in Turkey, 1980–1990.* PhD diss., Durham University 1995. In Durham E-Theses Online: http://etheses.dur.ac.uk/1158/

Mardin, Şerif. "Culture Change and the Intellectual: A study of the Effects of Secularization in Modern Turkey: Necip Fazıl and the Nakşibendi." In *Cultural Transitions in the Middle East.* Edited by Şerif Mardin, 189–213. Leiden: Brill, 1994.

Mazis, Ioannis. *Mystical Islamic Orders and Political-Economic Islam in Contemporary Turkey* [in Greek: *Μυστικά Ισλαμικά Τάγματα και Πολιτικο-Οικονομικό Ισλάμ στη Σύγχρονη Τουρκία*]. Athens: Proskinio, 2000.

Mazis, Ioannis. *Geography of the Islamist Movement in the Middle East* [in Greek: *Γεωγραφία του Ισλαμιστικού Κινήματος στη Μέση Ανατολή*]. 3rd edition. Athens: Papazisis, 2012.

Meeker, Michael M. "The New Muslim Intellectuals in the Republic of Turkey." In *Islam in Modern Turkey: Religion, Politics and Literature in a Secular State*, edited by Richard Tapper, 189–219. London: I. B. Tauris, 1991.

Mitraras, Aristotelis. *Anthology of New Turkish Literature: Poetry* [in Greek: *Ανθολογία της Νέας Τουρκικής Λογοτεχνίας: Ποίηση*]. Athens: Papazisis, 2015.

Okay, M. Orhan. *Necip Fazıl Kısakürek.* Ankara: Kültür ve Turizm Bakanlığı Yayınları, 1987.

Princeton Readings in Islamist Thought: Texts and Contexts from Al-Banna to Bin Laden. Edited and introduced by Roxanne L. Euben and Muhammad Qasim Zaman. Princeton, NJ: Princeton University Press, 2009.

Rahnema, Ali, ed. *Pioneers of Islamic Revival.* New updated edition. London: Zed Books, 2005.

Rahnema, Ali. *An Islamic Utopian: A Political Biography of Ali Shari'ati.* London: I. B. Tauris, 1998.

Rozanis, Stefanos. *Intellectuals and Modernity* [in Greek: *Διανοούμενοι και Νεωτερικότητα*]. Athens: Exarcheia, 2015.

Said, Edward W. *Representations of the Intellectual: the 1993 Reith Lectures.* New York: Vintage Books, 1994.

Şeyhun, Ahmet. *Islamist Thinkers in the Late Ottoman Empire and Early Turkish Republic.* Leiden: Brill, 2014.

Traverso, Enzo. *What Happened to the Intellectuals?* [in Greek: *Τί απέγιναν οι διανοούμενοι; Συζήτηση με τον Régis Meyran*]. Translated by Nikos Kourkoulos. Athens: Ekdoseis tou Eikostou Protou, 2014.

Uyguner, Muzaffer. *Necip Fazıl Kısakürek: Yaşamı, Sanatı, Yapıtlarından Seçmeler.* Ankara: Bilgi Yayınevi, 1994.

Watt, W. Montgomery. *Muhammad: Prophet and Statesman.* Oxford: Oxford University Press, 1964.

Yavuz, M. Hakan. *Islamic Political Identity in Turkey.* New York: Oxford University Press, 2003.

Zarcone, Thierry. *La Turquie moderne et l' Islam.* Paris: Flammarion, 2004.

Zürcher, Erik J. *Turkey: A Modern History.* 3rd edition. London–New York: I.B. Tauris, 2010.

Electronic media and newspapers

"Akit Yazarı Dilipak'tan Hilafet Çağrısı." *soL*, November 2, 2014, http://haber.sol. org.tr/devlet-ve-siyaset/akit-yazari-dilipaktan-hilafet-cagrisi-haberi-99492 (accessed May 8, 2015).

"Ali Bulaç." Committee to Protect Journalists (CPI). https://cpj.org/data/people/ ali-bulac/ (accessed January 12, 2019).

Dilipak, Abdurrahman. "Cemaat tek tip mi?" *Yeni Akit*, November 3, 2014. http://www.yeniakit.com.tr/yazarlar/abdurrahman-dilipak/cemaat-tek-tip-mi-8308.html (accessed December 30, 2015).

"Dilipak: Erdoğan Başkan Seçilirse Halife Olacak," *Yeni Akit*, October 25, 2015. http://www.yeniakit.com.tr/haber/dilipak-erdogan-baskan-secilirse-halife-olacak-102307.html (accessed March 30, 2016).

Hrant Dink Foundation, *Medyada Nefret Söylemi ve Ayrımcı Dil: Eylül-Aralık 2014 Raporu.* http://nefretsoylemi.org/rapor/EylulAralik2014raporuson.pdf (accessed December 30, 2015).

Hür, Ayşe. "Necip Fazıl Kısakürek'in 'Öteki' Portresi." *Radikal*, January 6, 2013. http://www.radikal.com.tr/yazarlar/ayse-hur/necip-fazil-kisakurekin-oteki-portresi-1115579/ (accessed December 28, 2013).

"Medyada nefret bilançosu: Yeni Akit zirvede,Yahudiler hedefte!" *Diken,* December 30, 2014. http://www.diken.com.tr/medyada-nefret-bilancosu-yeni-akit-zirvede-yahudiler-hedefte/ (accessed December 30, 2015).

Seufert, Günter. "Porträt Ali Bulaç: Jenseits von Konservatismus und Nationalismus." *Qantara.de.* February 16, 2007. http://de.qantara.de/inhalt/ portrat-ali-bulac-jenseits-von-konservatismus-und-nationalismus (accessed May 6, 2016).

"Turkey: 'Absurd' terror convictions of six journalists sends shock through media industry". Amnesty International UK. July 6, 2018. https://www.amnesty.org.

uk/press-releases/turkey-absurd-terror-convictions-six-journalists-sends-
shock-through-media-industry (accessed January 12, 2019).

"Türk Edebiyatının Çok Yönlü Şahsiyeti: Necip Fazıl." *Akşam*, May 24, 2012.
https://www.aksam.com.tr/kultur-sanat/turk-edebiyatinin-cok-yonlu-
sahsiyeti-necip-fazil--117635h/haber-117635 (accessed November 8, 2015).

"Two FETÖ suspects released in Zaman daily case." *Hürriyet Daily News,* May
12, 2018. http://www.hurriyetdailynews.com/two-feto-suspects-released-in-
zaman-daily-case-131706 (accessed January 12, 2019).

"Veysel Tepeli'nin Abdurrahman Dilipak ile yaptığı röportaj," *Adana Medya*,
May 29, 2009. http://www.adanamedya.com/veysel-tepelinin-abdurrahman-
dilipak-ile-yaptigi-roportaj-15345h.htm (accessed February 10, 2016).

"Ya Rab! Canımı İstanbul'da al!" *Yeni Akit,* October 5, 2014. https://www.
yeniakit.com.tr/haber/ya-rab-canimi-istanbulda-al-32217.html (accessed
February 10, 2016).

Index

INDEX OF PERSONAL NAMES

INDEX OF TERMS AND SUBJECTS